Columbia University Contributions
to Anthropology
Volume XXII

THE CUSTOMS OF THE BAGANDA
BY
SIR APOLO KAGWA

TRANSLATED BY ERNEST B. KALIBALA

EDITED BY

MAY MANDELBAUM EDEL

THE CUSTOMS OF THE BAGANDA

BY

SIR APOLO KAGWA

TRANSLATED BY ERNEST B. KALIBALA

EDITED BY

MAY MANDELBAUM EDEL

NEW YORK

COLUMBIA UNIVERSITY PRESS

1934

PRINTED IN GERMANY
J. J. AUGUSTIN, GLÜCKSTADT AND HAMBURG

Table of Contents.

56688

Preface.

This book was written in Luganda by Sir Apolo Kagwa,[1] regent and then prime minister, during the early part of the reign of Daudi Chwa, present king of Uganda. It was through him that Roscoe obtained most of the information that he used in writing *The Baganda*. This seemed an unsatisfactory account to the author of the present work, which is his attempt to improve upon it.

The most striking thing about it is that it is not, as we might under the circumstances have expected, an approach from a very different point of view, nor a presentation of facts startlingly at variance with those that Roscoe presents. Its organisation has clearly been influenced by that of the previous monograph, the picture presented is as completely formal, and the work as a whole reflects in no way the fact that the author was a participant in, and had intimate knowledge of, the culture he is describing.

This failure to tread significant new ground is to be explained by the fact that the author's conception of what an ethnological report could be was based on Roscoe's, and that he was writing in Luganda for an audience whose acquaintance with the culture he could assume. There may also have been reasons of state for this, particularly in the field of religion. Sir Apolo Kagwa was a professing Christian on good terms with the Church. It would have been an extremely jeopardous undertaking on his part to have revealed too thorough an acquaintance — of the sort he undoubtedly possessed — with unorthodox faiths.

What is presented here is, then, essentially an annotation and expansion of *The Baganda*. There are some new sections, such as those on games and songs; and the greater wealth of historical detail, particularly the lists of administrative officers since the time of the first king, is noteworthy.

This being the case, I have found it best altogether to omit such portions as coincide completely with Roscoe's account, and have indicated everywhere by brackets such duplications as had for purposes of intelligibility to be included. I have made parenthetic note of any apparent disagreements, and have indicated the

---

[1] Ekitabo / Kye / Mpisa za Baganda. / (The Customs of Baganda in the Luganda Language) / Kyawandikibwa / Sir Apolo Kagwa, K. C. M. G. / Katikiro we Buganda / Kampala: / Uganda Printing and Publishing Co., Ltd. / 1918.

omissions in this as compared with the original, as they occurred. The work of editing has included also phonetic retranscription of the native names with particular attention to the tones, which are so important in Luganda, though not usually included in the orthography. These have been appended to the translation in a list alphabeticallv arranged. Certain departures from standard spelling have been made even in the body of the text. Terminal syllabic m and v are written without the usual u. I have used tc for the affricate usually written ch, and ŋ for the velar nasal.

This work was undertaken at the suggestion of Professor Franz Boas. The editor acknowledges her indebtedness to him for making it possible, and also for his constant cooperation in the actual labors involved. The translation was done by Mr. Ernest B. Kalibala, a native of Uganda, with the assistance of the editor. Mr. Kalibala belongs to the Grasshopper clan, of which Sir Apolo Kagwa was also a member.

M. M. E.

CHAPTER I

THE COMING OF KINTU.

[Every Muganda knows that the first king of Baganda was Kintu, and knows the story of his coming.] (R. 186, 214, 460.) We shall start, therefore, with the traditions concerning his reign.

He had his court at Magoŋga hill in Busudju.

When the moon was about to appear the people gathered firewood for cooking and then at the appearance of the moon abstained from all labor for seven days. This rest was known as Bwerende. It was Kintu who first observed these days of honor to the moon, and after his death it became a national custom. At important temples of the gods people observed three days of rest after the appearance of the moon, and the king rested for one day, doing nothing but reviewing the fetishes, as a sign of his respect and gratitude at having been tided over another month. [Roscoe notes the same observance as performed in honor of one of the gods, Mukasa.] (R 299)

The building of Kintu's house was in charge of a man of the Lugave (manis) clan whose name was Kakulukuku. Twelve young men assisted. This house was only for Kintu and the royal property. There were ten houses about it for the women attached to the household.

When there was a feast [Roscoe says at the new moon] (428) Mwandje of the leopard clan took [six piles of cooked bananas and a goat and gave them to a man] of the Ŋkima (monkey) clan called Bwoya, [and a woman], Nanyeŋga, of the Nyonyi (bird) clan. [This food was left in the woods and it was found after sunset that it had been eaten by Kintu's children [Roscoe says Kintu and his son] (428) who were invisible princes and princesses......

No one but Kintu is buried at Nono. People were taken to their respective villages if they died there. But Mwandje had the privilege of burial there.

CHAPTER II.

KINTU'S ATTENDANTS.

These were the attendants during the reign of Kintu at Magoŋga. (Roscoe handles some of this material, from a different point of view, when dealing with clan legends.) (140 et seq.)

Mwandje whose clan was Ŋgo (Leopard), [was in charge at Magoŋga. Some members of the Leopard clan think that Keya son of Kintu was the father of Mwandje.] (140) Mwandje became the father of Namakaga and Serubambula. To these people the Leopard clan owes its origin.

Balasi of Monkey clan came with Kintu. When he came to Buganda he settled at Malaŋgala, in Busudju county, and became the father of Bwoya (Hare). When Bwoya became a mature young man, his father Balasi took him over to his master Kintu to act as page. When Bwoya [became a man he was honored with the office of Sabawali by Kintu. While he was holding this post his son Mulegeya was born.] (156) [Roscoe says Bwoya himself came with Kintu.] (156)

[Kisolo (Roscoe gives his name as Mwaŋgo) of Ɗoŋge (Otter) clan, came with Kintu. When he arrived in Buganda, Kintu appointed him Prime Minister.] (142) He settled at Bweza in Busudju. During this time he became the father of Lutaya, Seŋkuŋgu, Kiŋkumu. When Lutaya grew up he became Kintu's Sabadu.

[It is supposed that Kintu met Kadjoba (Roscoe calls him Ntege) in Buganda.] (145) Others think that he came with Kintu as his fisherman. He settled at Kanyanya in Busudju, and [became the father of Walusimbi.] When Walusimbi became a man he went to Baka where he became Sabadu during the reign of Tcwa Nabaka II. (146) When Tcwa Nabaka abdicated, Walusimbi undertook the administration of the Buganda Kingdom.

[Nyininseko] (R.'s Sesanga, owner of the jungle) [of the Ndjovu clan (Elephant)] is said by some to have been the son of Walusimbi, while others say he [came with Kintu. When they came into Buganda Nyininseko settled at Ntonyeze (R. has Sesanga) in Busudju.] (145) He had several children. His office was that of Kintu's chair carrier.

[Kaimbyobutega of Mpewo (Oribi) clan came with Kintu.] (157) When they came to Buganda he settled at Kiwawu in Busudju. His duty was birdtrapping. After his death his son Sekatampewo succeeded him. [Kiwuta Kyasoka of Mamba (Lungfish) clan came with Kintu. He was his brother.] (151) When they came to Buganda he settled at Mubaŋgo in Busudju. He became the father of Naŋkere and Mubiru. But Naŋkere affirmed that he himself came with Kintu, and Mubiru affirmed that he came from Bumogera to serve Kintu.

Bakazirwendo Semandwa of the Ŋgeye (Colobus Monkey) clan is said by some to have come in with Kintu, while others hold the opposite, saying that [Kintu found Bakazirwendo in Buganda.] (142) The former also hold that he was Kintu's brother-in-law. [His office was that of carrier of drinking water to Kintu.] (143) He became the father of Kasudju, after settling at Mubaŋgo. When he died his son was made the chief of Busudju at Mubaŋgo (R. calls Kasudju the first ancestor of this clan.)

Kakoto Mbazira (R. has Njuwe) of the Nyonyi (Bird) clan came with Kintu. (R. has him in Buganda first). (160) He settled at Luvunvu in Busudju. He was Kintu's personal doctor and [coffee cook[1].] (160)

Nsereko Namwama of Kobe (Yam) clan came from Masaba in Gwe (You) country to serve Kintu. He settled at Kanyanya, Busudju county. His office was that of a weapon maker. When he resigned, his son Mabiŋgo succeeded him. He went to reside at Buzimwa, Mawokota country. (R. says the ancestor of the Yam clan was Sedime.) (162)

Kyadondo (R. says he was Kintu's son) (158) of the Nvuma clan came with Kintu. He settled at Busaku, Busudju county. Here his son Kakoma was born.

[Mukibi Ndugwa (R. has Mukibi Sekiwunga) of the Lugave (Manis) clan was in Buganda when Kintu arrived] (153) Some people say he came with Kintu. [He settled at Magoŋga with Kintu,] and became the father of Kakulukuku. When his son became a full-grown man, he became Kintu's Prime Minister. Ndugwa himself settled at Wasozi.] (153)

[Kalibala of the Nsenene (Grasshopper) clan] came to serve Tcwa Nabaka. After Tcwa abdicated, he settled at Bala in Magoŋga. Other [people think that after he had separated from his elder brother he came to serve Kintu.] His office was to lead the way as an armed guard whenever Kintu travelled.

[Gadjule (R. has Nabuguza) of the Mbogo (Buffalo) clan came from Bunyoro with Kimera.] (154) Others say that he came with Kintu. When they came to Buganda he settled at Mubaŋgo, in Busudju. He was made Sabagabo, and was the father of Kaira.

Sensolo of the Ngabi (Bushback) clan came with Kimera. Some people think that he came with Kintu and settled at Magoŋga. His office was that of head cattle-man. He looked after Kintu's personal cow. He was also a doctor for setting dislocated bones.

These are the outstanding clans at Magoŋga up to the present. All these villages are in Busudju county. The lands each clan originally occupied are still distinguished.

CHAPTER III.

THE KING'S INAUGURATION.

The house called Buganda is so called because it is the house in which the newly elected king must sleep on the night of his election.

---

[1] Coffee was used in Baganda originally, though not as a drink. The roasted beans were chewed. E. B. K.

It was built by King Namugala, the first to pay the visit to Budo...
(104, et seq.)

In the march after the visit to Budo one of the stops was at a place
called Luiki near the court of Makamba, Budo chief. Here the king
selected an opponent for the checker-like game played by the Prime
Minister in the court house. This symbolized his ability to get the
best of any people opposing him, by wise direction of his government,
just as an expert player of this game can overcome his opponent
with a handful of reverse checkers.

There is a board with thirty-two holes for this game. Each of the
two players has thirty-two of the beadlike counters, which he
arranges, four to a hole in any set-up he likes. There is no real
resemblance to the European game of checkers. The counters in
the last two holes at the extreme left on either side, are called reverse
checkers, and have the privilege of moving in either direction......

Before the time of Namugala the princes had to go to Naŋkere to
be crowned. When he succeeded his father Mwaŋga he went to Budo
where he was advised to step upon the fetish, as all kings since
have done. He appointed Makamba and Semanobe, of the Mamba
(Lungfish) clan as guardians at the temple, and Naluŋga of the Manis
clan as overseer of other places in the vicinity.

It was thought that Budo told Namugala that it was upon that
very hill that his ancestor Kintu had beaten Bemba, the snake who
was the first king of Buganda. When Kintu killed him he became
king. That was why he urged Namugala to arrange that all his
descendants come to step upon the fetish in memory of the victory
of Kintu, before ascending the throne........................

[During the King's funeral rites Mbadja and Mugema sat opposite
each other at the royal fireplace and there burned a huge log taken
from the king's house.] (108) From this scene the Baganda made the
proverb,

"Beside the fireplace sit Mbadja and Mugema who failed to make
a fire for us." i. e. when a person is forced to do something, and his
heart is not in it, he will not do it well.

[Mugema was the chief honored with the task of dressing the king
for his enthronement. Mutebi changed this, giving the position to
Kasudju.] (198) Mugema retained the honor of burying the royal
corpses. At the death of King Mutesa the Prime Minister said to
Kasudju, "You have had the honor of dressing several of the kings.
Now Mugema must once more take over this office." As a result
of this it was the Mugema who hung the royal barkcloth upon
Mwaŋga II.

[When Kadjoŋgolo, Sabadu of Siŋgo, went to Bunyoro, he took

with him a prisoner and a piece of the log from the king's tomb] (206) known as the "little log". He killed the prisoner and burned him at a fire made from the log. This man was known as the "Fat Rooster killed during the king's ceremonies". Then Kadjoŋgolo attacked Bunyoro and returned with as much loot as he could get.

[For the rest the account here given agrees at least implicitly with Roscoe's, except that there is no mention of the "queen". Her existence is, however, attested in other sections.] (140 et seq., 189 et seq.)

CHAPTER IV.

BURIAL OF THE KING.

[Five months after the funeral and inaugural ceremonies, the king sends Kago, Sabaganzi, Mugema] and the police [to Merera to fetch the jaw of the dead king.] The officers stop off at Kitala or Sabaganzi, where some of the widows are stationed, but [the policemen fetch the jaw from Gundju of the Butiko clan]. (109) Sebata, Mpiŋga, and Mbadja are in this group.

When Gundju hands the jaw over to these men, he fetches the funeral barkcloth and they all enter the house. The body is then wrapped in this, and so covered over with barkcloth that the house is filled to its capacity. Then the door is shut and tightly fastened, and the pillars uprooted so that the roof falls down flat.

[.....The skull has the flesh eaten off it by insects and is then washed in Ndyabuwola, (a spring, not as in Roscoe's account a chief). The lower jaw is removed and washed with beer and milk to make it white.] (109) Kalogakalenzi is required to drink a mouthful of the second washing. Then he must say, "Here I give you the king, take him." The people answer, "The king has been drunk out by Kalogakalenzi."

This ends the funeral rites. Kalogakalenzi bids goodbye to the three policemen who have been playing a major role and they all leave for the city, stopping at Busawuli and Saŋganzira, and finally bringing the skull and separate jaw to the Kago and Sabaganzi.

[The jaw is washed in the same way on the next day and these officers drink of it.] (110) This is called "Drinking the King". Kago and the policemen then [polish the jaw... and store it in a wooden pan, which is put in a house specially built for it.] (110)

. . . .

The first royal burial was at Gombe in Bulemezi. Later it was transferred to Merera. These are the chiefs who play a prominent part in the royal funerals: Mugema, Sebata, Mbadja, Mpiŋga, Gundju, Lwabiriza, Kasudju, Kabanda, Makindu, and Seŋkaba.

They all have to be paid in advance, in women, cows, goats, and so forth. This all has to be paid by the newly-enthroned king. Mugema does not personally attend the funeral or come near the body.

When Mukabya became king he inquired of his chiefs as to the reason why these chiefs demanded to be paid in advance for these services. He was told that it was merely greed. Then he asked why Mugema who was identified with Nakazade, or the father of the king, did not attend the ceremonies. "Does he father only the living and not the dead?" he asked.

Then the king became very angry and ordered all the participants in the funeral ceremonies arrested and held for execution. Mugema, Kabanda, Makindu, and Sebata were not executed but merely deprived of their positions. This leniency was due to their age and their dignity among men. Mugema's office was given to Miingo of the Nsenene clan, the king considering this clan related to the royal one because Wanyana, mother of Kimera, was of this clan. He then demanded the following oath of his chiefs. "Upon my death you will bury me in the royal house, Muzib(u)-azala-Mpaŋga (The brave man begets a rooster) with my skull unmolested". Then he also ordered that the chiefs each be buried in the courtyard of his residence, and that the son who would succeed him found his city upon Nabulagala hill, and give orders, as for war, from the courtyard of what would then be the royal tomb. "If anybody claims to prophecy in my name, you must give him the Koran as an exposition of my disbelief in the whole matter." The chiefs gave their word to do these things should they live longer than he, and thus many obnoxious practices were done away with.

[It is believed by many that the custom of removal of the jaw began with Kalemera, who died on his way from Bunyoro. His attendants,] Lwabiriza of the Kobe clan, Kigu and Kalogakalenzi of the Fumbe clan, [cut off his head as evidence of his death.] (112) They laid it in the path of insects to clean it that it might be kept. When they brought it into the country a temple was built for it.

It is also thought that the body of Kalemera was not buried, but merely covered with plantain stems and left. The succeeding kings were treated in somewhat the same fashion, their bodies being covered with barkcloth and left in the tomb. The method of squeezing the royal bodies is said to have begun during the reign of Kaima. He was told about a very wealthy man in Budu and left upon a plundering expedition against him. On the way home he died of the plague. The chiefs squeezed the body now and again for fear of decomposition. The custom was then handed down. Some important chiefs and statesmen were treated in this fashion too.

The trouble with the theory that jaw extraction began with Kalemera lies in the discovery by the author of two jaws, tied in a bale of bark-cloth. The men in charge claim not to have known what was in this "unknown treasure" of Kintu's... The jaws are presumably those of Kintu and his wife Nambi Nantutululu or else of Tcwa Nabaka I.

Another theory accounts for the custom as associated with a belief that in returning to the other world these needed to be carried along.

CHAPTER V.

WORKS OF KINYORO.

Kinyoro of the Ŋkima (Monkey) clan gave the king his daughter as wife when he returned from the funeral ceremonies for his father and stood upon the throne in the royal gateway. He gave her to him as the traditional queen, saying, "I give you my daughter to prepare your meals. I also give you the whole of the Buganda kingdom." [By Roscoe's account the first queen married is one of the sisters of the king, who goes through all the coronation ceremonies with him, and the first woman given him after his installation is given him by Mugema.] (204)

Then he handed him the sceptre known as Bagambira, made of lusambya. [Roscoe says Semanobe at Budo gives him his sceptre.] (193) The king turned this over to his Prime Minister, saying, "Give judgment to all my subjects with this sceptre." Then Kinyoro charged the king to rule wisely. "Whosoever despises your honor, kill him, for all the peasants are like sorghum — whosoever mows it down, owns it."

For all this service Kinyoro was paid ninety each of women, servants, cows, goats, bales of barkcloth, and ninety cowries. Then he planted in the courtyard two trees which his father Mugema brought for the purpose. The long overlapping branches of these signified long life for the king. [Then the Prime Minister introduced all the chiefs again,] (204) and those who were made chiefs at Sanya had each to bring to the king one woman servant and one cow, and the rattles which were tied around the sceptre. These were all given to Kinyoro, who took them to Kibuye at Namuimba, and gave him nine items; he also gave nine items to his father. Then he returned to Busudju.

After three days Kadjubi of the Nsenene clan gave a girl, Nakimera, to the king... [Then all the chiefs and other people gave their best looking daughters, or other girls of their clans, to the king.] (204) Kinyoro sent a message to the chiefs of Budu, Katesigwa, Kadoli, and Kitaimbwa, to come to build a house for Nakimera.

When this was finished he sent to Muntu at Bwera and Wampandju at Mawogola for cattle to use at the ceremony for the opening of the house. The messenger took with him a spear known as Kanantai which belonged to the god Wamala, and was guarded by Kinyoro. When the ceremonies were over Kinyoro shaved his head.

Lady Nakimera was honored by several kings as representative of the Nsenene clan, whence Kimera had sprung. When she was still a bride she was given mutton, signifying that the original Nakimera was not a Muganda, but a Muima[1].

After a month Kinyoro ordered his son to collect reeds and make shields, and bring them to the royal gateway. They were given to Kago. He gave them to the king, who gave one reed and one shield to the temple of each of the gods. These were used in the building of the temples. They were to induce the gods to help protect the king against his enemies.

When the temples were all built, Kinyoro and Kago went to get the things for the dedication from the king. Kinyoro was then given the princess Nakampi to take to Nsambya. Here he gave her a sheep, and then in the evening jumped over her as she lay face downwards. This concluded the ritual of the temples.

After two days the princess went with him to Ndugwa of the Manis clan at Sekiwuŋga, who took her to Lusondo, chief priest of Wamala, and was given a sheep in exchange.

Finally the king asked Kinyoro to ask all the gods to prophecy for him. The priests were brought and stood before the king. They said. "You will live longer than all the other kings. You will be the father and all your subjects will love you dearly. Love the gods. They will defend your cause. Love your kingdom and be just. You will be more prosperous than the other kings and whenever you wage war you will win." This was the introduction of the prophets to the king. They were all given gifts and then the king left for Naŋkere's for the final ceremonies.

At first Kinyoro had only the task of giving the king a wife, signifying that the king was ready to marry. But one of them discovered and intercepted the plot to throw the jaw of King Djuko into the lake and was therefore considered to be a prophet, and given all these other duties.

CHAPTER VI.

THE KING'S CEREMONIES AT BUKEREKERE.

When the king was going to Naŋkere for the remaining ceremonies he went out of his way to go first to Bukoto in Kyadondo

---

[1] Baganda women do not eat mutton. E. B. K.

for hunting. Here he stayed one night and went through Kisasi, then Kumamboga, by way of Kasaŋgati, where he crossed the river, and came to Djita. He stayed here overnight and Djita gave him a girl, called Naluŋga. Then he travelled through Kabakuŋgu and came to Lulagala where he crossed the Mayandja river and came to the Busiro home of Nakuni of the Fumbe clan. When he left here he went through Koŋgodje and crossed Kabumba stream to Muzigo. Here he went to Kalonda of the Butiko clan, who said when he saw the king, "I have found. A finder is not killed." Then he took him into a special house. Kinyoro then went to tell Naŋkere where the king was. The next morning the king went to his house Nami-ryaŋgo, at Naŋkere which had two doors. The king entered from the front and Naŋkere from the back and they met in the center. [Then they exchanged beer jars in the presence of the queen mother.] (210) (Roscoe has only one stop on this trip — at a temple.)

The next night the king stopped at the house of Kalonda, and when he left he was met by Kikawa of the Ŋkima clan in Kambe. He robed the king in a barkcloth known as Eŋkaŋgabulu, which was pounded with a copper mallet on an ivory block. Then they both went to the house of Kasudju for the night......

After a few days, Kasudju and Nabitalo mounted the king on a stone known as Naŋfuka and showed him his kingdom. Kasudju said "I am your ancestor. My sister is the mother of Tcwa. That is why I am showing this to you."

Then the king left and crossed the Nakindiba river to Lugeye and Kidu's home, and then the Mulanda river to Buledza. He went to Nagaya, son of Walusimbi, who took him to Kitoke, to the home of his sister Naku, (Roscoe calls her the wife of Kidu) [where the king planted a plantain tree. .] (211)..........

At Kimogo the village of Walusimbi (which Roscoe calls a garden) (212) [after exchange of beer.]. . the blacksmith made three iron pot holders. They took these into the woods and used them to cook a meal of millet in brand new iron pots. The meal was ground by the daughters of Walusimbi. The chiefs then fed this to the king with triple branches. Walusimbi said, "I am the Sabadu of your grandfather Tcwa. You have brought me here to advise you as to the administration of your kingdom. I entreat you to be just, and kind to all but the disloyal." [Then the king and queen mother separated, for they were now both kings, and as such never allowed to see each other.] (210—213)

The next day the king went to Kiwembo and here a prisoner who had been arrested on the occasion of the game with Walusimbi was killed. The king then left and went to a well Nabaka and after drinking of it planted a tree near the well which he named Nsuka, as a symbol of his hope for a long life.......

[Next morning he] crossed the Kabumba river [into Kababi,] (212) where was the second court of the Mugema. He crossed the Wabitam river at the place known as Galinsaŋgawo, [where the cooking utensils were smashed] to rid the king of all iniquities, and diseases. On the other side of the river he met Kauzumo, the head policeman, who asked the followers, "You black-cheeked folk, didn't you paint the king black?" Anyone who dared to answer him was arrested and held for execution..... The king then went to Esaŋanzira, the home of princess Naluwembe. Here Kinyoro brought anklets he had made and these were put on the king by the princess. They were made of tiny glittering beads. Only the king wore such anklets. Walusimbi, Mugema, Gundju, Kasudju, and Naŋkere also wore anklets but theirs were of cowries and spinning tops.....

When men were sent for grass to build Naku's house, anyone who misunderstood and came back with any was beheaded and hung at the house. (Roscoe says, probably correctly, that only the first was so treated.) This man was known as "a young and careless grass-puller who will hit his elder." For bringing the grass back was equivalent to hitting the king with it. Then Naku prepared a feast for the king, bringing the water in iron utensils.

The next day the ceremonies relating to the ascension were all completed. The reason the king stayed a night at Naku's house was to get her advice on ruling the wives at the palace.

King Tembo is said to have been the first king to go through this ceremony before being hailed as the great king.

CHAPTER VII.

KINGS AND THEIR QUEENS.

[King Kintu had a wife named Nambi Nantutululu, daughter of Bakazirwendo, of the Ŋgeye clan. Their children were Tcwa Nabaka Wunyi, Mulaŋga, and so forth.] (214 et seq; 175 et seq.) However later the name Mulaŋga was changed to Kimera by Natigo of the Lugave clan.

It is thought by every Muganda that we are descendants of Kintu, his successor having given rise to the princes and all the rest of his descendants to the common people. That is the reason for the old saying "All Kintu's children did not perish." However, upon inquiry from the old people, we are informed that it was not Kintu who was the father of us all but that all the clans came into Buganda with him........(140 et seq.)

These were some of his important statesmen:

Prime Minister	Kisolo	Ŋoŋge clan; and
	Kakulukuku	Lugave clan;
Mugema	Bwoya	Ŋkima clan.

(A recent missionary report says that Kintu was a native of Southern Abyssinia, and that during the great tribal movement he happened to settle in Buganda. — E. B. K.)

Tcwa Nabaka I, the son of Kintu, married:

Naku, the queen, daughter of Walusimbi, of Fumbe clan, by whom he had no children.

Nakiwala, daughter of Semwaŋga, of the Ŋoŋge clan; son Kalemera.

When [Tcwa Nabaka succeeded his father Kintu,] (214) he founded his capital at Bigo hill. He built a house which he called Bugunya which means "chew slowly". He may have named his house so because he was fond of food.

These were the important statesmen:

Prime Minister	Walusimbi	Fumbe clan;
Kago	another Walusimbi	same clan;
Mugema	Bwoya, who held the position from Kintu;
Kaima	Kalibala	Nsenene clan.

[Prince Kalemera, the son of Tcwa Nabaka, had by Wanyana of the Nsenene clan], daughter of Mugalula Buyoŋga, [a son Kimera. Lady Wanyana was the queen of King Wunyi of Bunyoro. Prince Kimera was born at Kubulala.] (175; 215) When his mother visited Kalwayo village she had the permission of King Wunyi to visit her son and tend her millet crop. At this village were her brothers, Balitema, Kalanzi, Mpagi, and Masembe, who watched their own and their sister's cattle. Lady Wanyana had to go across a small stream, Kabaima, in order to get to her destination. The village where Kimera lived is called Mugabe, the plain in which the village is located is called Kigoyo, which is also the source of the Kitumbi river in Busenyi.

[King Kimera, the son of Kalemera, married three wives,

Wife	Father	Clan	Children
[¹Nabukalu	Ndugwa	[Lugave	
Naku	Walusimbi	Fumbe	[Lumansi
Namagembe]	Kaira	Mbogo]	Magambe.]

(175, 215, et seq.)

---

¹ Here and in all subsequent similar columns of names the brackets must be read vertically, that is, they open with the first name in the vertical column found in Roscoe, and close after the last.

2*

When Kimera ascended the throne, he founded his capital at Masanafu Hill. His house he named Kanyakasasa[1], which means "just as the blacksmith's shop has coal burning all the time yet no ashes accumulate, so it is with the king who always kills people and yet they go to him." His twin he named Lukungo, which means "The king has power over all the people." [When he died he was buried at Kanzige,] (216) whence King Mukabya removed his remains, and reburied him at Lunyo in 1869.

Kimera will always stand out in the memory. of the people because it was he from whom the present royal household descended....

These were his statesmen: Prime Minister, Walusimbi and Bakitunda, both of the Fumbe clan. Kago, Sebata of Ngeye clan. For Mukwenda, he appointed Gadjule of the Mbogo clan. Nabugwam Kakebe of the Mamba clan was appointed Kangawo. The Mugema was Katumba of the Nkima clan, who was the son of Mulegeya. Katumba during his childhood was brought up with King Kimera, his mother having been given charge of the prince. Balitema Kadjubi was appointed Kasudju. His uncle was Kodjawe of the Nsenene clan.

[Prince Lumansi, son of Kimera, married Natembo,] (135) daughter of Nankere of Mamba clan, [and their child was Tembo. He married Nadjemba,] daughter of Semwanga, Nonge clan. [Their children were Kigala, Lutimba, Nazibandja.]

When King Tembo ascended the throne, he founded his capital on Ntinda hill. He named his house Kiryoky(a)-embi-kyekiryokya-nenungi, which means literally, "That which will burn an ugly (house) will also burn a beautiful one." More freely it means that the king as well as the peasant will die.....

These were the important statesmen:

Prime Minister	Kiride	Kobe clan.
Kago	Sebata	Ngeye clan.
Kangawo, again	Nabugwam Kakebe	Mamba clan.
Mugema, again	Katumba	Nkima clan.
Kasudju, again	Balitema Kadjubi	Nsenene clan.

King Kigala Mukabya Kungubu, [son of Tembo, married six wives.

Nabukalu Nabuto,] (175) daughter of Natigo, [Lugave clan; child Kiimba.

Nakimera,] daughter of Masembe, [Nsenene clan; no children.

Nakauka,] daughter of Senfuma [Mamba clan; child Kasameme

---

[1] lit., blacksmith's forge.

Naku,] daughter of Walusimbi [Fumbe clan; no children
Nakyobula,] daughter of Mbadja [Mamba clan; child Gogombe.
Nawampamba,] daughter of Gundju [Butiko clan; child Wam-
   pamba.]

[When Kigala ascended the throne he founded his capital at
Kitala Hill.] (216) He named his royal house "A White Chicken".
This refers to the fact that a white chicken cannot conceal itself from
a preying animal, which can see it a long way off. Just so the king
can not conceal himself, but meets everything, public or private,
openly, whether or not it is good. He named his twin Lutimba[1]
(really the name of his brother), which means "The king is as a net
which is everywhere, and may kill you whether or not you go to
him". The king conquers not by himself but through those men
everywhere who support his cause, so that he triumphs over every
one of his enemies.

During his reign Kigala was beloved by his men as a fine and
gentle king. [He reigned until he was very old, when he asked and
received from his chiefs permission to resign in favor of his son. His
son soon died and Kigala Mukabya Kuŋgubu was again restored to
the throne.] (216) When he became very old and was almost blind,
his chiefs went into his royal palace and selected his best looking
wives. Since he could not see to distinguish among them his chiefs
took this advantage of him, and fell down on their knees giving
thanks for the women he had given them. At the same time his
most prominent wives gave girls away in exchange for the marriage
fee. [Eventually this good old king died and was buried at his capital
Mandja. His jaw was taken to Dambwe Hill] in Busiro.

These were his prominent statesmen:

Prime Minister	Kasoŋgov	Mamba clan
Kago	Sebata	Ŋgeye clan
Kaŋgawo	Kakebe, again	Mamba clan
Mugema	Katumba, again	Ŋkima clan
Kasudju	Sebatindira	Nsenene clan

[King Kiimba, son of Kigala, married two wives:
Bamugya] (175) daughter of Kisule [Ndjaza clan, no children;
Gwodjandjaba] daughter of Gundju [Butiko clan, no children.]

When [Kiimba became king] (216) he remained at Mpumude at
the capital of his father Kigala... Kiimba was a bad king. His
chiefs and all his people complained of his cruelty. When he heard
this he named his palace Koŋkomibi Lyerinanyini Kigagi, "An
ugly lizard is owner of the marshes." This means that whether a

---

[1] lit., long net.

prince is ugly, mean, or stupid makes no difference, he is still the king's son. He named his twin Wamala[1], which means, "Since you were crowned king, you have no need to worry, for everything is yours."

[Kiimba died before his father] and was buried at Lukwaŋgu, in Busiro. [His jaw was stored at Sentema Hill and his father was once more enthroned.] (216)

These were the important statesmen:

Prime Minister	Ntege	Fumbe clan
Kaŋgawo	Kakebe Nabugwam	Mamba clan
Kasudju	Sekizinvu	Ŋkima clan
Mugema	Luyombya	Nsenene clan

[Prince Wampamba, son of Kigala, married Nakaima,] (175) daughter of Gundju, [Butiko clan. Her child was Kaima.] It is said that this marriage was not justified because Nakaima was of the same clan as the mother of Wampamba. He was therefore given a name meaning "the wholesale swallower". Before her marriage to the king Nakaima had already born a son, Kauzumo.

Kaima, son of Wampamba, married:
[Nababiŋge] daughter of Wampona, Mamba clan, child Nakibiŋge [Nadogo,] daughter of Kasudja, Ŋgeye clan, child Kasabanda

When Kaima was crowned he founded his capital at Nanziga Hill. He named his house Kinyakyamulyaŋgo, "Doorway hole", which implies that though you may avoid falling into a pitfall while entering the house, you will not escape it again on leaving. The king referred to the death penalty. This also implies that the king ought to be brave in order to win against his rivals. Kaima is said to have been very brave and to have taken part, in person, in many battles. That is why he named his twin Katabazi, "Little Warrior".

[Once when the king was leading the army] against Bwakamba, a feudal chief at Nyendo [in Budu, he was killed. His remains were stored at Kibone in Buganda. His jaw was stored on Koŋgodje hill.] (217)

Before he became king Kaima took Nakaima's son Kauzumo as a policeman, to the rear of the house. There the instructed him in all the procedure related to the purification of a wife of the king after the death of any of her relatives. When he became king he appointed him to take charge of these observances in his own stead. He said, "When the fathers of my wives die, they will come to you upon their return from the funerals. You are my brother. Jump over them and shave their heads to purify them. I shall no longer bother." After the

---

[1] lit., that which finishes.

death of Kaima this became a traditional procedure. Each king appointed a Kauzumo to perform this ceremony of purification for him, which made it possible for his wives to return to the palace after attending a funeral. King Suna II modified this later, ordering that the belts be jumped over in place of the wives, and their heads be merely touched instead of shaved.

These were his principal statesmen:

Prime Minister	Sendikadiwa	Nsenene clan
	Walugali	Lugave clan
Kaŋgawo	Ziredja	Mamba clan

[Nakibiŋge, son of Kaima, married:

Wife	Father	Clan	Children
[Nabitaba]	Ndugwa	[Lugave	
Nadjemba	Semwaŋga	Ḍoŋge	Djemba
Naluŋga	Lusundo	Nvuma	
Namulondo	Gundju	Butiko	Mulondo
[Nasuna]	Naŋkere	Mamba	Suna] (175)
Bukirwa Nanzigu	Sekaiba	Mbogo	Nzigu
[Nanono]	Segirinya	[Ḍgo	Nono]

[When Nakibiŋge had won the contest with his cousin Djuma] (217) he founded his capital at Bumbu Hill. He named his palace Kanyakasasa and he named his twin Lukub(a)-egu[1], which means "Death takes the young people and leaves the useless old ones."

When Nakibiŋge became king many raids were made against Buganda. It is said that he went to Sese to ask Wanema to help him by enlisting more warriors. Wanema simply said. "If you want me to do this for you, you better leave your twin here that I may look at him." Nakibiŋge answered, "I shall send him here when I reach home." When he got back he took council with his chiefs as to how he should send the twin. He suggested cutting it in two, so that he could retain half. He named his part Kiteŋgo[2], "It is too heavy" because of the worry caused by his parting with it.

His wife Nanzigu was much honored by her husband because she consented to give her child to Wanema after his child was killed. Otherwise the king's twin left as security would have been jeopardized. Nakibiŋge willed a due honor to her just before he was killed. Mulondo became king and carried out his father's wishes. He built a separate house and enclosure for her. This was continued until the time of Mwaŋga when the introduction of Christianity weakened customs of this sort. However, when any prince is crowned her clan still brings Lady Nanzigu to the coronation as an honor to them.

---

[1] lit., smiter of the good.   [2] lit., a leopard trap

Lady Nanono was also honored. At the climax of a battle against the Banyoro the warriors all lost their spears. Nanono cut reeds to sharp points and gave these to the soldiers to use as spears. When the king was slain she retreated with the others to Bumbu. Here she remained for a year and a half as queen regent. She had just conceived when she went forth on the expedition. When she gave birth the child was a girl and did not live very long. Then, as she had no son, the chiefs proceeded to consider whom they should elect king. They finally consented to elect Mulondo. Lady Nanono remained at Bumbu, and it remains her property until to-day.

These were some of the statesmen during his reign:

Prime Minister	Kagali	Nvuma clan. When he resigned
	Kalumba	Fumbe clan
Kimbugwe	Namaŋgaŋgali	Fumbe clan, who resigned, giving place to
	Sendigya	Ndiga clan
Kago	Djita	Nvuma clan
Mukwenda	· Nakaswa	Mamba
Kaŋgawo	Ziredja, again	Mamba
	Nabugwam	
Mugema	Luima	Ŋkima
Kasudju	Lugendega, again	Nsenene

[King Mulondo, son of Nakibiŋge, married one wife, Naku,] (175) daughter of Nasereŋga, [of the Fumbe clan. She bore three children, Sekamanya, Walugembe, and Kazibwe.] (218) He also married four reserve wives..... He founded his capital at Mitwebiri Hill, and built his palace, which he called Kiryokyembi after that of his grandfather. He named his twin Makozi[1], which means that "he who does right is appreciated."

Mulondo was most erring in his conduct, and as a result he didn't live long. [When he died his body was carried to Gombe] in Bulemezi [He was the first of the royal family to be buried there. Recently Gombe] village was transferred to Kyadondo county, near Kuŋgu. His jaw was stored at his capital.

These were his statesmen:

Prime Minister	Sekagya	Nvuma clan
Kago	Sebata	Ŋgeye clan
Kaŋgawo	Ziredja	Mamba clan
Mugema	Namatiti	Ŋkima clan
Kasudju	Sendikadiwa	Nsenene clan

[1] I was unable to discover the literal significance of this name — MME.

King Djemba married:

	Father	Clan	Children
Nabandja	Kaira	Mbogo	Luļume; Kawali
Nakazi	Gabuŋga	Mamba	Gogombe
Naŋfuka	Kasudju	Ŋgeye	Zigulu

Djemba established his capital at Mubaŋgo Hill. He named his palace Bagambamunyoro[1], "Every evil thing is credited to the poor man's child while the child of the rich man is left free." He named his twin Waziba[2], "The person who puts barriers on the road and finds that someone has passed them is very angry." So it is with any enemy of the king. His hopes of promotion and honor are blocked.

Djemba was kind and gentle. When he died he was buried at Gombe. His jaw was stored at his capital Mubaŋgo, in Busiro. His statesmen were:

Prime Minister	Busaŋgwe	Ŋgeye clan
Kago	Sebata	Ŋgeye clan
Kangawo	Tabi	Mamba clan
Mugema	Maluge	Ŋkima clan
Kasudju	Sendikadiwa	Nsenene clan

[King Suna I, son of Nakibiŋge, married:
Nakigo,] daughter of Walusimbi, [Fumbe clan, child Sewati
Nalugwa,] daughter of Lwomwa, [Ndiga clan, child Kimbugwe.] (175)

He also married two reserve wives.

When he ascended the throne he founded his capital at Djimbo Hill, and named his palace after that of his grandfather. He called his twin Sekinyome-Kitwalaenswa[3], "When the driver ants destroy the edible ants, the one who is guarding the latter will guard them more carefully so that they will take away no more." So it is with the king. He is guardian of his people, and is careful lest anyone take them away.

He was kind and gentle and [when he died he was buried at Gombe. His jaw was stored at Djimbo, which had been his capital.] (218) He was reburied by Mutesa.

His statesmen were:

Prime Minister	Kisolo	Nsenene clan	He was also Kago
Kaŋgawo	Tabi	Mamba clan	These had served
Mugema	Maluge	Nkima clan	under Djemba
	Sendikadiwa	Nsenene clan, who had served	
		under Mulondo	

---

[1] lit., a derogatory nickname, "they call Munyoro".

[2] lit., that which fastens.

[3] lit., the big ant which takes the flying ants. A common derogatory nickname.

[Sekamanya, son of Mulondo], married:
[Nabuso Nabagereka,] (176) daughter of Gundju, [Butiko clan,
mother of Katerega]. He also married six reserve wives.

He established his capitol at Koŋgodje Hill and named his house
Kiryokyembi. His twin he called Nomerwa, "They do not like me."
He was cruel, and after violating the traditions concerned with the
assumption of the ruling power, he invaded and murdered Naŋkere.

[He loved his mother dearly and instead of having her establish a
separate home at Lusaka he built one for her] at Buswauli, [near
his capitol...]...(218)

These were his statesmen:

Prime Minister	Kisolo, again	Nsenene clan
Kimbugwe	Makabano	Mpologoma clan
Kago	Sebata	Ŋgeye clan
Kaŋgawo	Namukwa	Mamba clan
Mugema	Semukoteka	Ŋkima clan
Kasudju	Sendikadiwa	Nsenene clan, whom Mulondo had appointed.

[King Kimbugwe, son of Suna I, married Nakamyuka,] (176)
daughter of Mukusu [of the Mpindi clan, and had by her two
children, Kamyuka and Baleke. He also married Nakundja,]
daughter of Sekaiba, [of the Mbogo clan,] and seven reserve wives.

He founded his capital at Bugwanya and named his house the
same thing, which means, "We have come to-gether". His twin he
named Kyakulumbye Tekizikayo[1], which means that although you
pray hard death will claim you. He was a good king during his
reign. He died while at war with Katerega, son of Sekamanya, who
had resisted his power. He was buried at Merera and his jaw was
stored at his capitol. (R. says he was not buried, and had no
temple.) (219)

His statesmen were:

Prime Minister	Kamegere	Fumbe clan
Kimbugwe	Vudja	Kobe clan
Kago	Sebata	Ŋgeye clan
Kaŋgawo	Namukwa	Mamba clan
Kaima	Mpadwa, who failed to become king, but was a prince	
Kasudju	Sendikadiwa	Nsenene clan
Mugema	Semukoteka	Nkima clan

[Katerega, son of Sekamanya (176) married nine wives:]

Name	Father	Clan	Children
[Nakabugo	Mugema	[Ŋkima	[Lumansi Kidjodjo

---

[1] lit., it is hard to repel that which has already attacked.

Nakam	Kinyoro	Ŋkima	Naluwembo
Nakinyago	Naserenga	Fumbe	Kinyago
Nalongo Kawenyera	Mugema	Ŋkima	Waswa and Kato (twins)
Nalugwa	Lwomwa	Ndiga	Nazibandja, Seninde Gaweserwa
Namuyumba	Mugema	Ŋkima	Kauwa
Namugayi	Mpinga	Lugave	Kawaga, Kazibwe Katakesu
Namutebi	Mbadja	Mamba	Mutebi, Djuko, Kayemba
Nanzigu]	Sekaiba	Mbogo]	Nzigu][3]

He also married 100 reserve wives and had 200 maiden servants.

[Katerega distressed his step-father Kimbugwe by bringing with him for the completion of the twin ceremonies an ugly one of his wives instead of the beauteous Kawenyera who had borne them.] (218) Katerega then went to the Nonve river and there completed the ceremonial dances in connection with the birth of the twins. [Then he collected an army and proceeded to wage war against his stepfather. When he had gotten the best of him he became king.] He founded his capital at Lugeye Hill and built his royal house, Nakangu[1], "I hastened to become king." He named his twin Waziba[2], "He had blinded and eliminated all those who were hindering him from becoming king."

Katerega was a cruel king, but later he changed. He loved his warrior heroes. He appointed Maganyi to the office of Katambala because of his bravery, and in his will requested that this office and the county become the property of this man's clan. Up to the time of Mwanga II this was respected and the ruler of Katambala county was of the Ndiga clan. Balamaga of the Ntalaganya clan was also a hero. He was given the office of Kitunzi, and this remained in his clan until the time of Semakokiro...

His statesmen:

Katikiro	Kamegere	Fumbe clan, Kimbugwe's appointee	
Kimbugwe	Vudja .	Kobe clan	
Kago	Sebata	Ŋgeye clan	
Mukwenda	Kawewo	Nte clan	
Kangawo	Muvubi	Mamba clan	
Mugema	Semukoteka	Ŋkima clan, Sekamanya's mi- [nister.	
Kasudju	Ŋkune	Nsenene clan	
Kitunzi	Balamaga	Ntalaganya clan	
Katambala	Mpungu and Degeya	Ndiga clan.	

---

[1] lit., small, speedy, one.   [2] cp. p. 25, above.   [3] See note p. 19.

[King Mutebi, son of Katerega], married:

Wife	Father	Clan	Children
[Nabitalo	Walusimbi	[Fumbe	[Lukeŋge.
Nabukalu	Ndugwa	Lugave	Tebandeke, Nabuto.
Naluima	Nakatanza	Lugave	Kaima.
Namauba	Natigo	Lugave	Mauba, Mukuma, and Matumbwe.
Nampima]	Kibale	Mpewo]	Mpima.] (176)

He had also fifty concubines and a hundred maiden servants.

When [Mutebi became king] (219) he founded his capital at Muguluka hill and named his palace Kanyakasasa, like that of Nakibiŋge. He also named his twin Waswa Kazibwe. He was a wicked king and respected neither the landlords nor the chiefs. He tried to dismiss Kago, Mugema, and Sebata from office, but the chiefs kept him from this because of the precious dignity and honor of these men.

He gave the people of the Lugave clan the office of Kasudju, and he made Lubulwa of the Mpewo clan Saza chief. He also made Mudjaguzo drums known as Kaulugumo and appointed Lukuŋgo of the Lugave clan to beat them. He believed in and loved his gods and fetishes......

Statesmen:

Katikiro	Musezi	Fumbe clan
Kimbugwe	Sekade	Fumbe clan
Kago	Sebata	Ngeye clan
Mukwenda	Kawewo	Nte clan, Katerega's appointee
Kaŋgawo	Muvubi	Mamba clan, Katerega's appointee
Mugema	Semukoteka	Nkima clan, Sekamanya's appointee
Kasudju	Ŋkune	Nsenene clan, Katerega's appointee, dismissed
	Kalali	Lugave clan appointed
Kitunzi	Balamaga	Ntakganya clan Katerega's appointee
Katambala	Maganyi	Ndiga clan

[Djuko, second son of Katerega, married:]

Wife	Father	Clan	Child
[Nabatanzi	Sebugulu	[Lugave	[Batanzi
Nakimera	Kalanzi	Nsenene	Kimera
Nakisozi	Sekaiba	Mbogo	Kisozi
Naluŋga	Semalulu	Nvuma	Lumweno
Nandaula] Kabeŋgano,	Ŋkata	Nsenene	Ndaula
[Nantume]	Sekaiba	Mbogo]	Kasagazi] (176)

He also married seventy concubines and had one hundred thirty maiden servants.

[Djuko] (219) founded his capital at Ŋgalamye, and named his house Kanyakasasa, and named his twin also after that of Naki-biŋge. He was very wicked. He tried several times to destroy his brother Kayemba. Once he ordered him to sail in a clay boat. Instead he used a ·dugout canoe, went to Buvuma, and beat the Abavuma. He remained there for some time, until Mulwana, Djuko's prime minister, brought him back secretly to Buganda and hid him......

Djuko was the first of the kings to wear his hair in decorative crests.

Statesmen:

Katikiro	Wananda	Butiko clan
	Mulwana	Ḍoŋge clan
Kimbugwe	Luwaŋgalwambwa	Mamba clan
Kago	Kisolo	Nsenene clan
Kaŋgawo	Sendigya	Mamba clan
Sekibobo	Bwogi	Nsenene clan
Mugema	Semukoteka	Nkima clan, Sekamanya's appointee
Kaima	Bwogi	Nsenene clan, after he retired as Sekibobo
Kasudju	Kalali	Lugave clan, Mutebi's appointee
Kitunzi	Luzira	Ntalaganya clan
Katambala	Maganyi	Ndiga clan, Mutebi's appointee.

[Kayemba, Katerega's third son], married:

[Nabandja, daughter of Kasudju, [Ḍ]geye clan, [children Sematimba, and Wakaima

Naku,] daughter of Walusimbi, Fumbe clan], child Kaumpuli,] who was [badly deformed.] (219, 176)

He also married thirty concubines and forty maiden servants....

When he became king, he founded his capital at Lunyo hill and named his house and his twin after those of his brother Djuko, because they were sons of the same mother. However they never loved each other because of jealousy about the kingdom.

When Kayemba became king he was angry at his brother and also at his prime minister, whom he put to death. He ordered a policeman to throw both their jaws into the lake, saying, "Since he made a clay boat for me to sail in I shall do the same for him. Since you took council with him I shall drown you with him. He made me take you up on my shoulders. Now he will himself take you up." The men who

were given the jaws to drown got drunk and Kinyoro stole the jaws
and hid them. It was thus he acquired his prestige.

Kayemba ruled for many years and died of old age. His statesmen:

Katikiro	Kisiki	Butiko clan	
	Lugwanye	Fumbe clan	
Kimbugwe	Lutwama	Fumbe clan	
Kaŋgawo	Sendigya	Mamba clan	Djuko's appointee
Mugema	Semukuto	Ŋkima clan	
Kasudju	Kalali	Lugave clan	Djuko's appointee
Kitunzi	Luzira	Ntalaganya clan	Djuko's appointee
Katambala	Maganyi	Ndiga clan	Mutebi's appointee

[Tebandeke, son of Mutebi, married:]

Wife	Father	Clan	Child
[Nakyazirana Kadulubale	Sensalire	[Ndjovu	
Balaŋgaza	Sekaiba	Mbogo	[Djuma Katebe]
(Roscoe says Ekibanga)			
Nabali	Sempala	Fumbe	
Nabazika Kabedja	Mugema	Ŋkima	
Nakuwanda]	Mugema	Ŋkima] (176)	

Also thirty concubines and seventy maiden servants.

His capital was on Bundeke hill. He named his house Kanyakasasa, and he named his twin after that of Sekamanya. He was
wicked and bad-tempered. [He murdered all the gods, and then
became insane. When he recovered he himself started to prophesy
for Mukasa.] (220) When Seŋkaba, who had charge of the royal
tombs at Gombe, asked the king to provide him with a livelihood,
the king murdered him and looted the whole village. [Then he willed
that he himself should be buried at Merera. His jaw was taken to
Lunyo or Bundeke hill.] (220)

His statesmen:

Katikiro	Mudjambula	Fumbe clan	
Kaŋgawo	Sendigya	Mamba clan, Djuko's appointee	
Mugema	Sebina	Ŋkima clan	
Kasudju	Waŋkalubo	Lugave clan	
Kitunzi	Kiribata Malembo	Ntalaganya clan	
Katambala	Maganyi	Ndigo clan	

[Ndaula, son of Djuko, married:]

Wife	Father	Clan	Child
[Nabisubi,	Namenyeka,	[Mamba	
Nagudya,	Mukalo,	Ndjovu	Kagulu] Tebutwe-reke

Wife	Father	Clan	Child
Nakikulwe Nami- rembe	Kaindi	—	[Kikulwe
Nakide Luiga	Segirinya	[Ŋgo	Musandje, Mawanda, Ndege
Nakyomubi	Gabuŋga	Mamba	Kyomubi
Nampaŋga	Gundju	Butiko	
Nazaluno]	Walusimbi	Fumbe]	Bezaluno.] (116)

Also 200 concubines and 300 maiden servants.

[When Ndaula became king he suggested that instead of taking everything over himself his son Djuma succeed to the priestly side of his functions.] This was agreed to and Kaŋgawo appointed to take care of him at Kibaŋga village. [Now Djuma's descendants succeed with each new king.] (220)

He founded his capital at Lubaga and named his house Kasa- djakaliwano[1], "When a man who was held in respect dies his friends will speak well of him." He named his twin Lukeŋge, which means thorn, likening the king's power to a thorn planted in the earth. Any person passing by, unmolested by this thorn, is lucky. Just so pervasive is the king's power.

Ndaula was a kind and gentle king. He loved his people and ruled them peacefully. He was personally interested in his prime minister; so much so that in his will he specified that he be buried near him at the royal palace. [Ndaula lived to be very old. He died and was buried at Merera. His jaw was stored at Masaba hill.] (221) When his prime minister died he was buried there too.

These were his statesmen:

Prime Minister	Nsobya	Fumbe clan.
Kimbugwe	Kubira	Ŋgeye clan.
Kaŋgawo	Sendigya	Mamba clan.
Mugema	Sebina	Ŋkima clan.
Kasudju	Waŋkalubo	
Kitunzi	Kadjoŋgo, Nalumenya and Maseruka	Ntalaganya clan.
Katambala	Maganyi	Ndiga clan.

[King Kagulu] Tebutwereke, [son of Ndaula, had two children, Kaima and Sematimba, both of one wife,] whose name is not known. He founded his capital at Bulizo hill and named his palace Kasadja- Kaliwano after that of his father Ndaula. He named his twin Kyafubutuka. This means literally "it rushed" but actually it means "bad character". He was a very wicked king.......

[When he became king he murdered his brother and then his

---

[1] lit., the brave little man was here.

Mugema. Then he became a very vicious character.] (221) He ordered that the reeds be carried with the roots down and the tips up. This was very dangerous. He also ordered oak trees to be dug up with the roots no matter how deep these were. [He placed pikes wherever he held audience and made his subjects put their hands on these as greeting.] (221) He was therefore nicknamed Tebu-twereke, which means "intolerable". [Finally his subjects deserted him . . . .] (221). . . .

Then Kagulu decided to destroy his sister Ndege who was Nasolo. When she discovered the plot she told Kikulwe, Mawanda, and her other brothers and sisters. [They all decided to desert their brother and escape into Bunyoro.] (Roscoe says she took not her brothers but Musandje's sons.) When Namaba discovered their proposed flight he came to them and made a vow with Mawanda. [Namaba sheltered them until their brother Kagulu had fled from Buganda.] (221) When they returned none of them was free to assume the throne because Kagulu was still alive. Ndege left in search of him and found him drinking at Namaba's house at Kodja. She was to turn him over to her brothers and sisters, but so strong was her anger and desire for revenge that [she killed him and threw the body into a nearby lake,] (221) Bukule (Roscoe says Victoria Nyanza).

Nagadya's mother, when she was separated from her son, escaped to Sese, where she died.

Because of his wickedness Kagulu has no tomb at Busiro, and his jaw is not guarded and worshipped.

His statesmen:

Katikiro	Ntambi	Ndjovu clan, a close friend of the king's and equally wicked
Kaŋgawo	Kasalumuŋkandja	Mamba clan
Mugema	Sentoŋgo	Nkima clan
Kasudju	Nakaswa	Lugave clan
Kitunzi	Vunamuŋkoko	Ntalaganya clan
Katambala	Maganyi	Ndiga clan.

[Kikulwe, second son of Ndaula, married:]

Wife	Father	Clan	Children
[Nabido	Luba Musoga	[Nyonyi	[Mpalikitenda
Nadjuka	Gundju	Butiko	
Nakabugo	Mugema	Ŋkima	Madaŋgu, Nabaloga, Maganda, Gobaŋgo, Segamweŋge, Zansanze.
Namatovu	Kadjubi	Nsenene	Ŋgobe, Gomotoka]
Nantume]	Sekaiba	Mbogo] (177)	
Nanzigu			

He also married 250 concubines and 300 maiden servants.

When Kikulwe became king he was angry with and destroyed many people of the Ndjovu clan, whence Kagulu's mother had sprung. The remainder identified themselves with the Fumbe clan. Then he established his capital at Kibibi and named his palace Ndigalyamada[1], "He eats out of a garden when his brother who had invited him to eat is no longer there." (The implication is revenge.) He named his twin Luwuŋgwe[2], "Luckily the king missed me. If he saw me something evil would happen." In the olden days the result of meeting the king was death.

[Kikulwe was a wicked king. When he became king he tried to kill his brother Mawanda because he was jealous. . . . Soon Mawanda retaliated and killed him.] (221) He was buried at Luwoka and his jaw was stored at Kaliti hill. (Roscoe says at Busiro.)

His statesmen:

Prime Minister Mawuba   Mamba clan
       Nakiyendje   Butiko clan
       Nakikofu   Butiko clan
Mugema   Bisaso   Ŋkima clan
Kasudju   Nakaswa   Lugave clan, Tebutwereke's appointee
Kitunzi   Musoke   Ntalaganya clan
Katambala   Maganyi   Ndiga clan

[Mawanda, third son of Ndaula, married:]

Wife	Father	Clan	Child
[Kikome, Kadulubale	Gabuŋga	[Mamba	Beŋgo
Nabunya, Nasaza	Masembe	Nsenene	Mulere
Nabuso	Gundju	Butiko clan]	
Nakasinde	Namwama	Kobe	[twins Waswa, Nakato
Namisaŋgo	Sebugwawo	[Musu	
Naŋgnzi,	Mbazira	Nyonyi	Kirabe
Naŋkonyo]	Kagenda	Mamba]	Namirembe.] (133)

He also married 203 concubines and 300 maiden servants.

When [Mawanda became king,] (222) he founded his capital at Katakala hill and named his house Kiryokyembi, after that of Tebandeke. He named his twin Simbwa[3], meaning that he was appointed that all the people might bow down before his honor.

He was extraordinarily fierce, brave, and tyrannical. He waged war upon and ravaged the Basoga. Up to date they call any king of Buganda Mawanda. Then he dismissed several chiefs, including Nabugwam who was Kaŋgawo, Kago, and Sekibobo. He appointed several heroes of the war to these vacant offices.

---

[1] lit., I shall eat it when I return.   [2] lit. ,luck.   [3] lit., the great one.

3

[Several of the children of Musandje later fought with and killed him.] (223) Then they hid his body. It was found several days later and sent to Merera for burial. In 1860 Mutesa took this, and the jaw which was stored at Serinya hill, and buried them at the latter place.

His statesmen:

Prime Minister	Sebanakita	Mamba clan
Kimbugwe	Kavuma	Nvuma clan
Kago	Mpembe	Lugave clan ·
Sekibobo	Ŋkalubo,Sebugwawo	Musu clan
Kaŋgawo	Matumpagwa	Ŋkima clan
Mugema	Mugwanya	Ŋkima clan
Kasudju	Lubiŋga	Lugave clan
Kitunzi	Madjweŋge	Ntalaganya clan
Katambala	Maganyi	Ndiga clan.

Musandje, fifth son of Ndaula, married:

Wife	Father	Clan	Child
Bauna	Magunda	Fumbe	
Nabulya Nalugwa	Lutalo	Ndiga	Mwaŋga, Namugala, Kyabagu.
Namirembe	Semateŋgo	Ndiga	Kayondo.

Also ten concubines and thirteen maiden servants.

His son Mwaŋga was king. He married:

Wife	Father	Clan	Child
[Nadjuma	Natigo	Lugave	[Mulage. He was made Sabadu of princesses and it was with him that the twin ceremonies were performed.
Nakabugo	Mugema	Nkima	Kiwanuka
Nakiwala (Omubika)	Semwaŋga	Ŋoŋge	
Nalubowa	Segirinya	Ŋgo	
Namakulu]	Mpiŋga	Lugave	Nkondogo].

When he became king there were 100 reserve women and 390 maiden servants. He retained all of them because his reign was short and he had no time for the regular process of selecting wives... He was buried at Merera (Roscoe says Busiro) and his jaw was stored at Kavumba hill, in a house called Kuŋanyi, "It was the king who gathered together both good and bad men. That is why they fooled him and caused his death." His twin was called Walugya[1], "You are responsible for your death." Mutesa reburied him at Kavumba.

His statesmen:

Prime Minister	Sebanakita	Mamba clan
Kaŋgawo	Matumpagwa	Ŋkima clan
Mugema	Magwanya	Ŋkima clan
Kasudju	Lubiŋga	Lugave clan
Kitunzi	Kakale	Ntalaganya
Katambala	Maganyi	Ndiga clan

[Namugala, second son of Musandje, married:]

Wife	Father	Clan	Child
[Basuta Kadulubale	Masembe	[Nsenene	
Nadjuka	Gundju	Butiko	[Katerega
Nakaŋgu	Kagenda	Mamba	Ŋgabo
Nalubowa	Segirinya	Ŋgo	
Naluŋga	Terwewalwa	Nvuma	
Nawaguma]	Kisule	Ndjovu]	Kaboli.] (177)

Also fifty concubines and 100 maiden servants.

Namugala started the tradition of going to stand on Budo's fetish. He founded his capital at Nansana hill and named his house Kin-ya-kya-mulyaŋgo[2], "You may escape a hole in the doorway in the morning but you will fall into it in the evening." So it is with escaping the king's death penalty. He named his twin Lukaŋga, "chastiser."

Despite his drunkenness he was a lovable king, and merciful ruler. [His brother insisted on having Diboŋgo Omutamanyaŋgamba killed as the murderer of their father.] (224) To save his friend Namugala invaded his village, killing over two hundred people but saving him. [Later he quarreled with his brother and retired in his favor,] going to Mawokota in Bulamadzi. Once after a visit to his brother he slipped and was killed. He was buried at Merera and his jaw stored at Muyomba hill. Mutesa reburied him in 1869.

His statesmen were:

Prime Minister	Kagali	Nvuma clan
Kaŋgawo	Kambugu	Nyonyi clan
Mugema	Mugwanya	Ŋkima clan
Kasudju	Lubiŋga	Lugave clan
Kitunzi	Kakale	Ntalaganya clan
Katambala	Butekanya	Ndiga clan

---

[1] lit., that which takes away.   [2] lit., doorway-hole.

3*

[Kyabagu, the brother who succeeded him, married:]

Wife	Father	Clan	Children
[Gwolyoka	Myamba	[Lugave	[Nsekere
Kiribwa	Sebugulu	Lugave	
Magato	Namukoka	Mamba	
Misiŋga	Natigo	Lugave	Sanya
Mbigide	Terwewalwa	Nvuma]	
Nabiweke	Segirinya	Ŋgo	
Nabugere	Sekaiba	Fumbe	Mbadjwe
Nagalale]	Lule	Ɖoŋge	Nalukwakula
Nadjemba Omubika	Lule	Ɖoŋge	
[Nalubimbi]	Namwama	[Kobe]	Saku
Nalugoti	Masembe	Nsenene	
Naluŋga	Lugundju	Nvuma	
[Nalwondoba	Naŋkere	[Mamba	Waŋgo
Namayanya	Bude	Mamba	Sekafuwa, Kiribata, Kikunta
Nambowoze	Namwama	Kobe]	Twins, Kalema and Kigoye
Naŋkandja	Nakabalira	Nvuma	
Nanteza]	Kakembo	[Ndjovu]	Djundju, Semakokiro, Kyomubi, Zansanze]
Nfambe	Sekaiba	Fumbe	(178)

Also 300 concubines and 400 maiden servants.

[He immediately seized Diboŋgo and killed him.] (224) The country resented this. He founded his capital at Lubiya hill and named his house Bunonya[1], "I enjoy my kingship." He named his twin Mutebi after his grandfather Mutebi.

Kyabagu was a gallant and brave man who conquered the whole tribe of Busoga. He was strong and stout, but a trifle short. His head was bald down to the ears. The people composed the following song about him:

> Since his desertion from the kingship
> Behold his white grayed head
> Despite his white grayed head
> He is a strong man.

During his reign the royal sacrificial places for the slaughter of princes were established. These were Busenyi and Namugoŋgo.

[Eventually his sons murdered him and he was buried at Merera

---

[1] lit., the looked-for.

and his jaw stored at Gombe.] (225) In 1869 Mutesa reburied both
at Kyebando.

[The reason for his murder (from *The Kings of Buganda*, p. 64.)
is this:

Once his shepherd,] Bwafama, [let his cattle stray upon the
pasture of Prince Sekafuwa, who warned him against letting this
happen again. A few days later he brought them down again. They
grazed there, and trampled the remainder under foot. Again the
man was warned, and when he did this for the third time, Sekafuwa
was angry and seized and killed a cow. When it was prepared he
sent a piece to his mother. This enraged the king. [He seized Sekafuwa's mother, slew her, and placed her on the road], lying on her
back. [Then he invited all the princes to an audience with him.
Sekafuwa led the group which set out, and saw and recognized the
corpse of his mother.] He covered his eyes, and after covering the
body with his outer garment he returned home. The next day
Sekafuwa, Kikunta, and Kiribata secretly plotted to take revenge
upon their father. When they heard that Nabukome had come to
carry out the ceremonies relating to the birth of twins, they followed
him. Kikoso, a servant of Nakirindisa, Sekafuwa's uncle, [murdered
Kyabagu. In the upset Nambowoze, one of the king's wives, was
forced to murder two men.] (224)

His statesmen:

Prime Minister	Kabinuli and Lugolobi	Nvuma clan
Mukwenda	Mutumba	Kobe clan
	Kabugo	Mbogo clan
Sekibobo	Nakyedjwe	Nyonyi clan
Kaŋgawo	Kambugu	Nyonyi clan
Mugema	Walulya	Ŋkima clan
Kasudju	Ŋkuse	Lugave clan
Kitunzi	Fambaga	Ntalaganya clan
Joint rulers of Budu	Kauli, Bulanda and Bwakamba	
Katambala	Kyoka and Nadjumwa	Ndiga clan

[Djundju] (225) son of Kyabagu, married:

Wife	Father	Clan	Child
[Katagya Nakam]	Gabuŋga Lwomwa	[Mamba Ndiga	[Kyomubi Semalume]
[Nakam Tebwaza]	Katambala Kasamba	Ndiga Mbogo] (178)	

Also 200 concubines and 400 maiden servants.

He founded his capital at Mugoŋga in Busiro, and named his house after that of his grandfather Mawanda. His twin he named Tauta[1], "a king never becomes stupid, even though he be old. Whatever he says is accepted with pleasure by his subjects, and those who do not do so are disloyal."

Djundju was a great and brave man [who subdued all of Budu and Kiziba.] Here the Baganda were nicknamed Abayundju. He was a cruel king, and murdered several people. [He hated his younger brother Semakokiro, though Semakokiro had saved his life and kingdom by killing] Mukuma who [had risen against him...] (225)...

Mayembe, his prime minister, whom he loved dearly, used to remain with the king in order to cover him with his blankets, and only then return home. For fear of him the people could not revolt against the hated king. Some of them reported to the king an oracle which proclaimed danger to him unless the guards killed anyone they saw passing through the court early in the morning. This was arranged, and so they rushed upon and killed Mayembe on his customary early morning journey. [Then the plotters took council with Semakokiro, who fought against and killed his brother, and became king.] (225) A song was composed for this occasion:

> Confide in no man
> They with false evidence to Djundju
> Murdered Mayembe.

He was reburied by Mutesa.

Prime Minister	Sendegeya, Mayembe and Kagenda	Mamba clan
Mukwenda	Kairikita	Mbogo clan
Kaŋgawo	Kambugu	Nyonyi clan, Namu-gala's appointee
Mugema	Kyeusa	Ŋkima clan
Kasudju	Ŋkuse again. Also Ŋkuse II, Gagaŋga I and II, and Naŋkere.	All Lugave clan Ntalaganya clan
Kitunza	Kabuzi	
Pokino	Iga and Luzige	Ndiga clan
Katambala	Nadjumwa	Ndiga clan

[Semakokiro, second son of Kyabagu, married:]

Wife	Father	Clan	Child
[Ndwadewazibwa	Luyombo	[Nsenene	[Kamanya, Ndagire]
Balambi	Sembudze	Ndiga	Nakuita

---

[1] lit., let him not become stupid.

Wife	Father	Clan	Child
Bawede	Nakato	Mbogo	Luyendje
Bwaita	Djumba	Ŋkima	Tebatagwabwe
Guluma	Lusiŋga	Ntalaganya	Nabisalu
Gwowoleza	Luzige	Ndiga	Mutebi]
Djadjawabana]	Serusa	Ndiga	Mutebi
[Kikubula	,	Luzige	Ndiga
Nabisunsa	Mukusa	Mpindi	[Nagadya
Namatama	Malunda	Ndiga	Zimbe
Sebandabawa	Ŋkali	Ŋgeye	Kiyumba
Sirisa]	Sikiwede	Mamba	Kakirebwe
Siyainza	Djumba	Ŋkima]	Kakuŋgulu] (178)

Also 1500 reserve wives and 7000 maiden servants.

When Semakokiro became king he founded his capital at Kasaŋ-gati in Kyadondo. He named his house after that of Djundju. He also named his twin after one of his ancestors — Lumansi. He is said to have had a fine personality and to have been very handsome. He had full, round, shiny eyeballs, and a fine light black body. He was also very brave. He was very reckless and cruel when he came to the throne, but changed after reigning for some time. As soon as he was crowned [he had three of his children and some of his brothers' killed. They were burned alive, ostensibly because they had formed a conspiracy against him.] (226) He also murdered a number of the members of the Mamba clan who were supposed to have been implicated in the death of Djundju. Those of the members of the clan who managed to escape identified themselves with other clans. Some of them are known as Abakunta. They escaped by way of Busagala and settled in Nalugulu.

Once he seized Ndwadewazibwa, mother of Kamanya, Bunya, Sepuya, and several others. They were sent to Mutuŋgo, where they were drowned in the Victoria Nyanza. But he was not yet satisfied. He seized his son Kamanya and put him to work cutting down trees at Kasaka, hoping that the unaccustomed hard work would kill him. This failed, however.

While he was at his capital Kitende a bird known as Kimbagaya lighted on his house. He issued an order at once to seize all the members of the bird clan immediately and execute them. He really thought that they had in some mysterious fashion ordered this bird on his house. There is a proverb which says, "You have brought upon me that which Kimbagaya brought upon the Balama."

This is used when anyone gets into trouble and suspects another of having caused it. The Balama symbolize any people who cannot defend themselves. Here the reference is to the members of the bird clan who were executed for a supposed offense.

When he had executed the members of the bird clan he discovered his mistake and repented of what he had done, and as a result he became a good ruler and was beloved of his people. They began to undertake commercial enterprises which brought in wealth and his chiefs actually were obeyed when they suggested cessation of execution.

[When he died his body was buried at Merera, and his jaw entombed on Kisimbiri hill.] In 1869 Mutesa reburied him.

These were his statesmen:

Prime Minister	Nabuŋga,	Ndiga clan
	Sekaiba Nabembezi	Mbogo clan
	Kiyanzi	
	Kaduwamala	Nvuma clan
Kimbugwe	Kinenenyumba	Lugave clan
Kago	Ŋkali	Ŋgeye clan
Mukwenda	Nakato	Mbogo clan
Muwemba		
(Mukwenda)	Sepuya	Nsenene clan
Sekibobo	Ziziŋga	Musu clan
	then Katumba	Mbogo clan
Namutwe	Kireŋge	Nsenene clan
	then Nsimbi	Mamba clan

The latter was one of the men who fought for Mutebi when he was warring with his brother Kamanya.

Kaŋgawo	Bunya	Nsenene clan
	Sekono Magere	Nyonyi clan
	Makya	Butiko clan

All the sons of Bunya became important chiefs. They were Kadjubi Senteza Kamunyi; Kironde; Kidza; Nteyafa; Luyombya; Sebowa.

Mugema	Bandabalaga	Ŋkima clan
Senkezi, assistant Mugema	Wamala	Ŋonge clan
Kaima	Bwete	Mamba clan
	Sepuya	Nsenene clan

Kasudju   Nandere, then Waswa
                and then Nandere II,
                Wamala   all Lugave clan.
                Nakato succeeded them   Mbogo clan
Kitunzi   Mukokera,   Kobe clan
Pokino   Luwalira,   Ndiga clan
                Wananda, a prince   Fumbe clan
                Zibukuimbwa
Katambala   Kiube, Kakono, Seru-   Mamba clan
                biri, and Sekigude   Ndiga clan

[Kamanya, Semakokiro's son,] (178) married:

Wife	Father	Clan	Child
[Bakuira	Lule	[Ŋoŋge	[Kigala
Basima	Katesigwa	Ŋkima	Nakibiŋge
Gwowemukira			
(a Muhima)			Kimera Kigala
Head Wife			Ndaula Kiterera
			Lule
Kayaga	Kiwalabye	Kobe	Babirye and Nakato
			— twins
Kisirisa]	Lutaya	Ŋoŋge	Kagwa
Samanya [Kiza]	Walusimbi	Fumbe]	Nakibiŋge]
			Baunyakaŋgu
[Kyosibyomunyoro	Djumba	Ŋkima	[Mbadjwe
Kyotowade	Kiyaga	Mamba	Bamweyana,
			Mugogo
Kyowolofude	Lutalo	Ndiga	Nakayeŋga (and
			Nanjade — R.)
Lubade	Madjandja	Ŋgeye	Tadjuba, Nama-
			yandja
Mpozaki] Mukoki	Katesigwa	Ŋkima	Nabaloga, Twaise
[Mubyowuwo	Nakatanza	Lugave	Nasolo, Kagere
Mutezi	Nakato	Mbogo	Nambi
Mukwano	Mugema	Ŋkima	Kyomubi
Nambi	Lutaya	Ŋoŋge	Nakaŋgu
Nabikuku	Djemba	Ŋkima	Nasolo] Mwanyi-
(Kabedja)			nempologoma
Nabirumbi	Kisule (Busoga)	Ndjaza	[Nalumansi
Nabiswazi	Djumba	Ŋkima	Luwede
Nabiyoŋga	Myamba	Lugave	Naku
Nabowa	Kafumbir-	Lugave	Kimera
	waŋgo		

Wife	Father	Clan	Child
Nakadu	Kamyuka	Mpindi	Lumansi, Namika
Nakanyike	Senfuma	Mamba	Tebandeke
Nakazi Kanyaŋge	Sambwa Katenda	Mamba	Suna II
Nakazi	Lutalo	Ndiga	Wasadja] who was buried at Kibwa
Naku	Walusimbi	Fumbe	[none
Nakyekolede	Gabuŋga	Mamba	Ndaula, Mutebi
Nalumansi	Walusimbi	Fumbe	Nakalema
Namala	Kyewalabye	Kobe	Kigoye
Namauba	Sempala	Fumbe	Ndagire
Namukasa	Naŋkere	Mamba	Kigala
Nambi Tebasanide	Mugula	Mamba	Waswa, Babirye — twins; Kadjumba; Mbadjwe
Namwenyagira	Kamyuka	Mpindi	Nakabiri
Nanozi (princess)	Gomotoka		Ndagire
Naŋkandja	Terwewalwa	Nvuma	Nasuna Kyeteŋga
Nzalambi	Natigo	Lugave	Kidza, Nakayeŋga
Siribatwalira (Muziba)		Ŋkima]	Katalina Mpalikitenda Nabisubi
Tebemalizibwa]	Myamba	Lugave	Nagadya]

Also 1000 reserve wives and 9963 maiden servants.

Lady Gwowemukira was said to have been the head wife during the reign of Kamanya, and to have had fifteen children, but the names of them have been lost.

There were three princesses who were highly honored. Tadjuba daughter of Lubade, was most honored. She outlived most of the others of her father's children. (She was consulted by the author, in writing of her family.) Mwanyinempologoma and Katalina Mpalikitenda Nabisubi were also honored and longlived. The latter became a convert to Christianity before she died. This book was written during the later part of her life.

In 1790 [Kamanya became king] (226) He founded his capital at Nsudjumpolu hill. He named his house Kasadjakaliwano, after that of his grandfather Ndaula. He named his twin Sebukule[1], "great", meaning that the dignity and honor of the king are greater than those of any of his subjects.

Kamanya was of medium height, light skinned, with fine eyes. He had a low but nice voice, but sometimes slurred his words. He

---

[1] lit., let them develop.

was a brave man and desired to expand his kingdom. He therefore organized several expeditions which followed one another in rapid succession so that the men were always in the field. He himself did not take part in the fighting. His wars came to be known as "restless warfare", because the men were not permitted to rest and even children of fourteen were required to carry each his two spears and shield to war. By this means he widened the bounds of his kingdom, which was pressed in by the Banyoro.

On the whole Kamanya was a thoughtful king. He is remembered for the many gifts he gave his people. [But despite his generosity he had bad traits. One is shown in his arresting his son Nakibiŋge] Baunyakaŋgu and the boy's mother Samanya and ordering them both [to be killed.] (226) They were taken to Busonyi in Busudju; Samanya was killed first and then Nakibiŋge was severely handled. Finally he was put between his mother's legs and coldly murdered, and then burned. After this Kamanya was stricken and paralyzed on one side. He died in 1810 and was buried at Merera and his jaw stored at Kaseŋgedje hill. Mutesa reburied him.

Prime Minister	Kaduwamala	Nvuma clan
	Katimpi	Nvuma clan
	Kafumbirwaŋgo and Kimoga	Lugave clan
	Sebuko	Mamba clan
Kimbugwe	Ndjaleruma and Sikyawoza	Ŋgeye clan
Mukwenda	Mulalira	Kobe clan
	Mpaŋgala	Ŋkima clan
	Mandwa	Mamba clan
Kago	Sekyeri and Sekade	Butiko clan
Sekibobo	Kitumba	Nyonyi clan
	Sebude	Nvuma clan
	Wakizige	Fumbe clan
	Kanamalansendja	Mamba clan
	Sewaŋkambo	Ŋkima clan
	Kabiswa	Musu clan
Kaŋgawo	Kirimutu and Bigomba	Ŋgeye clan
	Nabwaga	Nvuma clan
	Mandwambi	Ŋkima clan
	Muguluma	Fumbe clan
	Gombe	Ngabi clan
Mugema	Sewanonda and Kibalama	Ŋkima clan

Kaima	Luima	Nsenene clan
	Lwaŋga	Musu clan
	Bekaleze	Nsenene clan
Kasudju	Wamala	Lugave clan
	Kyasima and Basadja-ŋkambwe	Lugave clan
Kitunzi	Luziŋgo	Ntalaganya clan
	Kigwe	Mamba clan
	Mpeŋgere	Mpewo clan
	Musudja	Ŋgeye clan
	Nteyafa, son of Bunya	Nsenene clan
Pokino	Prince Kabwa	
	Kabuzi	Ŋkima clan
	Kidza	Nsenene clan son of Bunya
Katambala	Kiube,	Mamba clan
	then Sebanakita and Senteza Kamunyi,	Mamba clan

son of Bunya and father of Kalanzi Kironde, Kadumukasa, Kidjala, Saloŋgo, etc. Kadumukasa is the father of Apolo Kagwa, Kiwuwa, Kafumbe, Kirigendali, all Ndiga clan.

Luwekula established when Kiwalabye conquered Buwekula and became Sabawali of Mukwenda's county. The people were afraid of him at first, keeping children away. They nicknamed him Luwekula[1]. From that time the name Luwekula indirectly applied to Kiwalabye. Up to these days every successor is known by that name. Kiwalabye was a great man in his day. He had a son who is reputed to have been braver than his father.

King [Suna II,] (179) Kamanya's son, married a hundred and forty-eight wives.

Wife	Father	Clan	Child
Alibatakyaye	Nakatanza	Lugave	Nagadya
Alibulira	Ndugwa	Lugave	Nalumansi, Nawati, Nende
Bageyeramunaŋge	Sekadjidja	Ndjaza	Kalimuduŋgu
Bagwanya	Lukoda	Ndjovu	Kyomubi, Mirim, Ndaula, Wamala

---

[1] meaning, the snatcher.

Wife	Father	Clan	Child
Baita	Mugema	Ŋkima	Ndikyabya, Beŋgo, Tewa
Bakazibagya	Mpisi	Ŋgabi	Mukeka
Bakedja	Namaguzi	Mpologoma	Madzi
Bakwanya	Sendikwanawa	Musu	Mpologoma, Dje-mba
Baŋkebera	Gundju	Butiko	Lubambula
Basude	Senyondo	Kobe	Kawaga, Luwede
Buisi	Kawali	Ŋonge	Nakayoŋga
Bukodjaŋge	Setyabula	Fumbe	Nakamanya, Kadjumba
Bulisa	Mukusu	Mpindi	Nasuwa
Bwamutuka	Kiwanuka	Ŋonge	Namika
Guliko	Mbazira	Nyonyi	Tebugwa
Gwaiŋga	Kasudja	Ŋgeye	Lukoŋgwa, Magu
Gwendisaŋga	Mugema	Ŋkima	Lulunda
Gwerude	Nsumweku-lubye	Ŋgeye	Mukundja, Kale-mera, Mbowanye
Gwewadjokulaba	Madjandja	Ŋgeye	Nzigu
Gwokebera	Kasudja	Ŋgeye	Kagumya
Gwosuza Muzoŋgola		Ŋgeye	Kikulwe
Gwotonabanaye I	Kawali	Ŋonge	Kagere
Gwotonabanaya II	Lule	Ŋonge	Binanyegera, Lu-waŋgiza
Itaneba Nantume	Namige	Mbogo	Mukuma, Djuko
Kabakalindjulira	Katenda	Mamba	
Kabakaloŋgosa	Semwaŋga	Fumbe	Mukabya
Kabakandjagala	Kasudju	Lugave	Kazibwe
Kabigya	Lule	Ŋonge	Ndege, Nakake
Kadja	Gundju	Butiko	Nakalagwe
Kalaba	Mugema	Ŋkima	Kayondo, Nakyo-bula
Kantamaga (Muima)	Mugema	Ŋkima	Bwakoba
Kanyoro	Kaliro	Fumbe	Magembe, Nakyo-bula, Kayemba
Kayaga I	Semwaŋga	Fumbe	Goloba
Kayaga II	Kaima	Mbogo	Kaima, Nalya-kuŋgabo
Kayaga III	Kaima	Mbogo	Kaima
Kayaga IV	Kaima	Mbogo	Wakaima
Kiboyanye	Lule	Ŋonge	Zalwaŋgo

Wife	Father	Clan	Child
Kiitire Banawa	Mabundugu		
[Kikolwamuganzi] (Kadulubale)	Mpagi	[Mbogo]	[Lukaŋga, Wampamba, Kato, Nawati, Babirye]
Kikome I	Semwaŋga	Fumbe	Gulubagwire
Kikome II	Katambala	Ndiga	Mbadjwe, Nagadya
Kikome III	Kikandja	Lugave	Nandaula, Baina
Kiragadja	Mugomba	Lugave	Nakanaku, Muinda
Kiribwa	Sebuko	Mbogo	Kigoye, Ndagire
Kiride (Nasaza)	Mpagi	Nsenene	
Kitambuza	Sebaduka	Mpindi	Damali Ŋkizi Nawati
Kizala I	Mugema	Ŋkima	Natu
Kizala II	Gombe	Ŋkima	Leya Kibali Natu
[Kubina]	Magunda	[Fumbe]	Noho Kyabaseŋga [Mbogo]
Kuwekitibwa	Ndugwa	Lugave]	Kiryewala
Kyabaŋgi	Sekaiba	Mbogo	Sekamwa
Luvamubaima	Semwaŋga	Fumbe	Kadjumba, Waswa, Kato, Koko, Nsindjo
Makerere	Sekaiba	Mbogo	Nalumansi
Mikisesaŋgwa	Gundju	Butiko	Watuyo
[Mirika Balaguza] Kafude	Nanyinigutwe	[Lugave]	[Dina Namirembe]
Mubisi	Musitwa	Butiko	Nandaula
Muganzabulirwa	Mabundugu	Mbogo	Ndagire
Muganzamala Kuwona	Sekaiba	Mbogo	Mbadjwe
[Muganzirwaza]	Galabuzi	[Ndjovu]	[Mukabya] Walugembe Mutesa]
Mukulukyayogera	Kaliyisa	Ŋkima	Musandje
Mulaŋga	Gabula (Musoga)	Ŋgabi	Mulaŋga
Mutandalyomumwe	Namudjulirwa	Ndiga	Mulekwa
Muzairwa	Mugema	Ŋkima	Kigala
Muzibukulaba	Walusimbi	Fumbe	Kyabasiŋga
Mwagale	Kàduwanema	Nsenene	Muinda, Nakazana
Mwanyinamwomi	Namwama	Kobe	Mawanda Nantale
Mwaza (Muima)		Ŋkima	Baliza

Wife	Father	Clan	Child
Nabaliyo	Sekaiba	Mbogo	Tezira Nsaŋgi
			Lumama
			Sekanyo
			Kaima
			Sanya
[Nabamboŋge	ʼMagunda	[Fumbe]	[Serwola
(Kabedja)]			Nasolo Kyebutula]
Nabiiki I	Mugema	Ŋkima	Maindja
			Bamweyana
Nabiiki II	Mugema	Ŋkima	Luswata
Nabikoni	Luwekula	Kobe	Nasuna
			Salome Bagambani
•			Kiimba
			Ndjera Nandjera
Nabitwere	Mukusu	Mpindi	Walugembe
Nabosa	Katambala	Ndiga	Kimera
Nagadya I	Magunda	Fumbe	Djemba
Nagadya II	Walusimbi	Fumbe	Nsereko
Nagadya III	Lukoda	Ndjovu	Tonsera
Nagyawa	Gabuŋga	Mamba	Segamweŋge
Naita I	Lukokera	Kobe	Djemba
Naita II	Setuba	Kobe	Djemba
Nakadu	Lukoda	Ndjovu	Kimbugwe
			Mutebi
			Wakyama
			Mpewo
			Wakaima
			Nasimbwa
			Nabweteme
			Nsaŋgi
			Sanya
Nakalema	Mbazira	Nyonyi	Mwaŋga
Nakalyana	Katologo	Ndjaza	Lumansi
Nakapoki	Nakatanza	Lugave	Nsereko
			Mulondo
			Namayandja
Nakasala	Mugema	Ŋkima	Nakigala
			Lugyayo
Nakibuka I	Nakatanza	Lugave	Kasadja Mulekwa
Nakibuka II	Myamba	Lugave	Luvule
			Lukwakula
Nakidjoba	Myamba	Lugave	Genza
Nakim	Kasudju	Ŋgeye	Luwede

Wife	Father	Clan	Child
[Nakiwala]Sabadju	Lule	Ɖoŋge	[Kiwewe]
Nakimera	Senteza Ka-munyi	Nsenene	
Nakomo I	Terwewalwa	Nvuma	Mayendje
Nakomo II	Terwewalwa	Nvuma	Ndagire
			Mayendje
Nakutanya	Kinyoro	Ɖkima	Wasadja
			Nakayeŋga
Nakyawa	Kagenda	Mamba	Nende
Nalisaŋga	Kaliyisa	Ɖkima	Masanafu
Naloŋgo I	Setyabula	Fumbe	Nsindjo
Naloŋgo II	Setyabula	Fumbe	Kadjumba
Nalubale	Mukusu	Mpindi	Musandje
Nalugwa	Namudjulirwa	Ndiga	Musandje
Namaga	Sendikadiwa	Musu	Waŋgo
Namakula	Mutyaba	Lugave	Genza
Namirembe I	Kasudja	Ɖgeye	Koko
Namirembe II	Nsamba	Ɖgabi	Musulo
Namusoke	Walusimbi	Fumbe	Sekadakiro
Nambi I	Katambala	Ndiga	Zansanze
Nambi II	Kibugo	Ndiga	Mutebi
Nambi III	Gabuŋga	Mamba	Simbwa
Nambi IV	Kasudja	Ɖgeye	Nakiwala
Namwagala	Walusimbi	Fumbe	Wakibugu
			Namalwa
			Wasadja
Naŋkya	Kyewalabye	Kobe	Nambi
Nantume I	Kaira	Mbogo	Nalumansi
			Kayemba
Nantume II	Sekaiba	Mbogo	Mukuma
			Djuko
Nasozi	Tondo	Ɖkima	Zansanze
			Nakyobula
Nundayalusi	Djumba	Ɖkima	none
Ndibulwam	Kakinda	Kobe	Mawemuko
Ndimugambako	Nakato	Mbogo	Lakeri Semusamba
			Sikyagatema
			Katulume
Ndimukwasa	Mbazira	Nyonyi	Kyomubi
Nfunda I	Kaira	Mbogo	Kubite
Nfunda II	Mugula	Mamba	Waŋgo
Ɖgubi	Namwama	Kobe	Kiwala
Ndjalegwa I	Walusimbi	Fumbe	Tebandeke

Wife	Father	Clan	Child
Ndjalegwa II	Magunda	Fumbe	Tebandeke
Nyonta	Walusimbi	Fumbe	Namulinzi
			Muyendje
Simunenya	Kyaze	Mpindi	Bamweyana
Siribaganya	Mukusu	Mpindi	Mudondoli
Siriko	Mugema	Ŋkima	Nandaula
			Nakuita
Tagambwako	Setuba	Kobe	Kakuŋgulu
Takolakabi	Kaira	Mbogo	Mugale
Talikogwakyaye	Mbazira	Nyonyi	Kyesoŋgera
Tatugiriraŋge	Kyewalabye	Kobe	Tebandeke
(Omuwaŋga)			Namugayi
			Kalikuwona
Tegutukwako	Madjandja	Ŋgeye	Nambi
			Walulio
Tezira Lugugule	Kabadzi	Kasimbi	Nakato and
			Waswa, twins
Tuitenaye	Mbazira	Nyonyi	Nawati
Tukemala	Kasudja	Ŋgeye	Kimbugwe
			Alizabesi Ntaleye-
			wera
			Babirye and
			Nakato, twins
Tebandowoza	Mugema	Ŋkima	Njobe
Mugema			
Twogere (Omu-	Sekaiba	Mbogo	Bandanyemu
womya)			
Wabulenseko	Ndagala (of	Ŋkima	Namawuba
	Kalagwe)		
Wogundeta	Kaira	Mbogo	Nyinzi
Wanyana	Kadjubi	Nsenene	Walulio
Watasima	Kasudja	Ŋgeye	Tutekubano
[Wozako (Omuko-	Senteza Ka-	[Nsenene]	[none]
kiro)]	munyi		
Yabuwaŋgula	Ndugwa	Ndugwa	Nabasasanya
Yanteka (Muima)			Bateŋga
Zagwa	Kyewalabye	Kobe	Kyesuluta
Zawede	Magunda	Fumbe	Nabaloga
			Nabada
			Kikulwe
			Ntege
Ziribwaga	Luwekula	Kobe	Wakasaŋke

4

He also married two thousand reserve wives and eighteen thousand maiden servants.

Lady Kiitire Banawa was a princess and childless. When her husband died she lived a secluded life away from men. She would not re-marry, shake hands with a man, or enter a man's house. She spent the rest of her life in mourning.

Damali Ŋkinzi, daughter of Kitambuza, was the queen sister of Mukabya. When Christianity was preached in the country she took a great interest in teaching the people about her to learn to read and write.

Mbogo, son of Kubina, was very badly treated. When queen-sister Muganzirwaza murdered all his sisters and brothers by starving them, he was arrested and placed in prison for eight days without a drink or a mouthful of food. However, he and his fellow-prisoner, Maindja, were freed. Maindja was put to death during the reign of Kalema, but Mbogo escaped this penalty, and some days later accompanied the king to Kidjuŋgute village, where he died. Mbogo was appointed king by the Mohammedans. It was then (1890) that Captain Lugard made his appearance. He invited all the Mohammedans to return from Kidjuŋgute. They did, but in 1893 after their revolt, Mbogo was exiled to Zanzibar by Lugard. He was exonerated and freed after two years, but he returned to Uganda only to find that all his followers had scattered. However, he gathered together those whom he could and lived in amity with the people again. They still regard him as their religious leader. (Mbogo died in 1923). We were honored in securing a great deal of information from him. He was a well-informed gentleman, who survived his brothers and sisters and was honored for his willingness to entertain everybody.

Maindja, son of Lady Nabiiki I escaped the death penalty with Mbogo but was later burned by Kalema when the king was at his capital Nakatema.

Lady Ndimugambako kept all men from her, barring even the baby boys from her home, when her husband died. She spent the rest of her life mourning for him.

When Suna became king in 1810 he founded his capital at Mulago hill. He named his house Batandabezala — "Kings beget Kings" — the word Batanda being a term of dignity. He named his twin Lumansi after that of Semakokiro.

Suna was only about twelve years old when he succeeded to the throne. He was a peaceful and able ruler for many years. There is a song about this: "Suna is a peacemaker, he will make the children grow." Later he changed and became a cruel king. The song too was changed: "King Suna will ruin himself."

He was very handsome. He had beautiful eyes, and a commanding voice. He was also brave, but he was excessively interested in women, having more wives and children than any of his predecessors. He also did a great deal of hunting, and was very cruel and excessive in his slaughtering. He loved his relatives, and as he didn't like to be in public places, invited them to visit him. He appointed his brother Sabaganzi, "the best of my friends", and another Ŋkobe, "he who encloses". He was also very fond of his fathers-in-law, with all of whom he conversed. They were privileged to look at him as long as they liked..... Hunters too were allowed to approach and talk to him, and never suffered if they announced the finding of the trail of an animal which was not successfully hunted.

He was fond of his prime minister Kaira. Once he returned from a campaign in Busoga and the king had everybody drink the beer which was stored in a jar called Kawulula. The general tasted and drank first, and then called the king Semunywa, "archdrinker" because he had drunk all Busoga country. The king in turn named Kamalabyona, "the one who is final in all matters", for his definitive subjugation of the Basoga. When the king was thus named he created a butler's office and appointed Kasindula of the Ŋgabi clan, who was a Munyoro, Munamweŋge.

Suna was a cruel but firm and able king. [He died in 1852 and was buried at Merera. His jaw was stored at Wamunyenye or Wamala, his capital.] (227) Here Mutesa reburied all his remains.

Prime Minister	Migekyamye	Ŋgabi clan
	Kaira	Mbogo clan
Kimbugwe	Mutyaba	Lugave clan
	Kidza	Nsenene clan
	Nyamaŋka	Lugave clan
Kago	Sikayanira ⎫	
	Damulira ⎬	Lugave clan
	Nyamaŋka ⎭	
	Bulega	Musu clan
	Lwaŋga	Fumbe clan
Mukwenda	Sentuka	Mbogo clan
	Kantinti	Ŋkima clan
	Bakabulindi	Ŋgeye clan
	Nyamaŋka	Lugave clan
	Nduga	Fumbe clan
Sekibobo	Kantinti	Ŋkima clan
	Kabulindi	Ŋgeye clan
Kaŋgawo	Wemirira	Fumbe clan

4*

Kaŋgawo	Ndolombe	Musu clan
	Mpeŋgere	Kobe clan
	Kyagaba ·	Butiko clan
Mugema	Sekitoleko, Busagwa Senyamantono, Miiŋgo, Nakabale	Ŋkima clan
Kaima	Mbabali ⎱ Nantagya ⎰	Nyonyi clan
Kasudju	Basadjaŋkambwe Ntambazi Sebitosi Lubiŋga Nakaswa Mutagubya Seŋkoto, and Kabidzi	all Lugave clan
Kitunzi	Nakamali and Sekikoŋge	Mbogo clan
Pokino	Semukuluŋgwa	Ndiga clan
	Kigwe	Mamba clan
	Mabale	Fumbe clan
	Omuziŋga	Musu clan
	Namudjulirwa	Ndiga clan
Katambala	Kabula	Ndiga clan
Luwekula	Setuba	Kobe clan

[Mukabya Walugembe Mutesa, son of Suna, married:] 179)

Wife	Father	Clan	Children
Kavebukasa	Mwerumubi	Ŋgeye	S. Nakalema, wife of S. Luluga Kakuŋgulu
Bulya	Kasudju	,,	Ŋkinzi
Gumenya	Bakabulindi	,,	Luswata, Kikulwe
Kalibwa	Kyoto	,,	Bateŋga
Nagadya	Kyoto	,,	Waŋgo
Munaŋambalira	Madjandja	,,	Nakibiŋge
Nakibuka	Mabundugu	,,	Natu (Nabulebwe)
Nambadjuwe	Ŋkondo	,,	Genza
Tagusenda	Kalinda	,,	Namukabya
[Abisadji Bagalayaze]	Sekimwanyi	[,,]	[Danyeri Mwaŋga]
Bulya	Kiwanuka	,,	Baliza
Nampa	Kiwanuka	,,	Katerega

Wife	Father	Clan	Children
Kireberebe	Lule	Ŋgeye	Kimbugwe
Kuwandikira	Lule	,,	Kalemera
Kubweyuna	Lutaya	,,	Genza
			Nakamanya
			Lubuga
Nawati	Lutaya	Ɖoŋge	Tebandeke
Muleba	Kidza (Pokino)	Nsenene	Mutebi
Mukomutanda	Mugema	Ɖkima	Kagere
Namukasa	Mugema	,,	Walulio
Sai	Mugema	,,	Sekanyo
Mugoloba	Djumba	,,	Dzimbe, Bamweyana
Nantaba			Batanda Ntege
Nakanwagi	Galusandja	Ngabi	Zansanze
Nakasolya	Tukube	,,	Nabweteme
Sabadju	Nsamba	,,	Mbiro
Balaŋgirabazala	Sekaiba	Fumbe	Nawati

(Lady Balaŋgirabazala was a noted musician and knew well how to sing accompanying songs.)

Wife	Father	Clan	Children
Namirembe (Kadulubale)	Sewaya	Fumbe	Nabanakulya, Nasimbwa Asiyati
Buganzikiruŋgi	Mbadja	Mamba	Ndaula
Bulyama	Muwemba	,,	Nyendje
Bukirwa	Gabuŋga	,,	Nsindjo
Kikome	Gabuŋga	,,	Agiri Namirembe Lubuga
[Kiribaka	Gabuŋga	[,,	[Kiwewa
Ndibuwakani]	Gabuŋga	,,]	Kalema]
Kiwagi	Munyologanze	,,	Magembe
Kwazika	Kamakya	,,	Tɔwa
Sagalambule	Kamakya	,,	Sanya
Yakindowoleza	Kamakya	,,	Lebeka Mugale
Luŋkireribaze	Semanobe	,,	Lubuga, Nende
Namayandja	Kisomose (Katikiro)	,, ,,	Wampamba
Namusoke Namayandja		,,	Ntege
Nansove	Ɖkambwe (Kaima)	,,	Lumama
Nanteza	Kigonya	,,	Mulondo
Ntembo	Mabundugu	,,	Lugyayo
Tusuza	Kagenda	,,	Kyomubi

Wife	Father	Clan	Children
Wavuvumira	Ŋkaŋgi	Mambe	Katerega
Namusisi	Mutoŋgole	,,	Djuliya Nakayeŋga, Lubuga
Alindjidjukira	Nandere	Lugave	Mbiro
Alyemalenyandja	Mayandja	,,	Bagambani
Bulimwomuganzi	Ndugwa	,,	Nambi
Kyawera	Namugwaŋga	,,	Nantale
Nagadya I	Bisobye	,,	Nalumansi
Nagadya II	Serundjogi	,,	Nawaŋku
Namakulu	Nyamaŋka	,,	Kimbugwe
Namale	Kasudja	,,	Goloba
Namirembe	Kadjoŋgolo	,,	Nasuswa
Nambi	Damulira	,,	Wasadja
Kyagera	Gundju	Butiko	Bagambani
Mirisiyane Bulimweŋgo	Musitwa	,,	Segamweŋge
Naŋkya	Lugundju	Nvuma	Kadjumba
Fenayatedza	Namakaga	Ŋgo	Nawati
Nakibuka	Seŋkole	,,	Namauba
Kawanvu	Lutalo	Ndiga	Lumama, Ndagire
Namukasa I	Ntensibe	..	Wakaima
Namukasa II	Basiga	Mpewo	Genza
[Gwomuruŋgide (Kabedja)]	Mukindikira	[Kobe]	
Buteseza	Mabirizi	,,	Luwede Nabaloga
Nsibuka	,,	,,	Kasadja
Mukeŋgo	Mpeŋgere	,,	Kikulwe, Naluwembe
Yatwandjulira (Omusibika)	Namwama	,,	Baizi
Nakigozi	Sebugwawo	Musu	Nakim
[Nabagereka (Kadulubale,)] a princess	Dagane	[Nvuma]	
Bukirwa	Mukude	Mbogo	Lukaŋga
Kadugala	Kaira	,,	Mpologoma
Nakibuka	,,	,,	Lugomye
Kikome	Makumbi	,,	Kayondo Kyomubi
Mukomulwanyi	Bakamempisi	,,	Nakabiri
Nakadu	Mpindi	,,	Nasuswa
Nawagi	Kiriba	,,	Mukuma

Wife	Father	Clan	Children
[Kaliŋganyana]	Seŋkatuka	[,,]	Namulinzi [Kimera]
Namagembe (Omusibika)	,,	,,	
Bulya	Mbazira	Nyonyi	Natu
Yazaula	,Kyasima	Mpindi	Nasolo Zalwaŋgo
Kabayoŋga	Mutatembwa		Nakanyiga
Omulabirawala (Munyoro)	Muziba		Katerega

He also married a thousand other wives and had seventeen thousand reserve wives.

Nsibuka, after the death of her husband secluded herself, particularly from men, whom she did not even allow to enter her house. The marks made upon her chest by the tears she shed were long visible. She ceased to shave her hair, and cut it only when it became so long that it covered her eyes.

When Mukabya became king in 1852 he founded his capital at Nakatema hill and called his place Muzib(u)-Azala-Mpaŋga[1] which means "The king is the rooster and the subjects are the hens." He named his twin Sebukule, after that of Kamanya. He also named it Bakumbanamulam[2], "Let the dead mind their dead." Living people are not interested in the dead.

Mukabya is said to have been very tall and dignified. He had a Roman nose, beautiful eyes and brows, and a well-balanced neck. He was very well loved by his subjects. Because [he was unusually intelligent](227) his prime minister Kaira named him Mutesa. When he became king some of the officers plotted in secret to remove him and make another member of the royal family king. When Mutesa became aware of this situation he captured these men and had them put to death. Then Kaira gave him this name which means "the one who is fine in council matters."

During this campaign he was also known as Mukabya, "the one who makes others cry". He destroyed several who had taken arms against him. He was extremely young, and the people feared that the task might be too much for him. He therefore plunged into various activities to prove his abilities. When he grew older his people loved and respected him. He was well-disposed towards his subjects. [During his reign several foreigners came into the country and he treated them well.] (229)

---

[1] lit., the brave man begets a rooster.
[2] lit., they walk with the living.

[The country was progressive and prosperous.] Many people owned live stock which they housed in their dwellings.

[He was the first king to be converted to Christianity.] He commanded that all his subjects do likewise. He died in October, 1884, after an illness of several months, and during this time Apolo Kagwa was a page in the butlery and served all the medicine to the king.

[When he died he was buried at his capital, Nabulagala or Kasubi, without the removal of his head.] He had succeeded in reburying the collected remains of ten of his predecessors by then.

His officers were:

Katikiro	Kaira	Mbogo clan
	Kisomose	Mamba clan
	Mayandja	Ŋkima clan
	Mulere	Ndjovu clan
	Mukasa	Musu clan
Kimbugwe	Madjandja .	Ŋgeye clan
	Luka Sekamwa	Mpewo clan
	Tebukoza	Lugave clan
Kago	Kisomose	Mamba clan
	Bawalesanvu	Nsenene clan
	Kabirinage and Kiwanuka	Ŋgeye clan
	Kaya	Mpewo clan
Mukwenda	Munyologanze	Mbogo clan
	Kabirinage	Ŋgeye clan
	Bawalesanvu	Nsenene clan
	Mubiru	Butiko clan
	Dumba	Mbogo clan
	Kabuŋga	
	Kiyega	Mbogo clan
Sekibobo	Misalenyoka	Mbogo clan
	Kaya	Ŋgeye clan
	Kirabira	Mbogo clan
	Bawalesanvu	Nsenene clan
	Mandwambi	Lugave clan
	Magimbi Kamanyiro	Ndjovu clan
	Mukasa	Musu clan
Kaŋgawo	Kadu	Ntalaganya clan
	Sebowa	Nsenene clan
	Nyikomunyoŋga	Mamba clan
	Namalele and Kibiraŋgo	Lugave clan

Mugema	Ŋkakalukanyi	
	Malagala	
	Kolokolo	
	Musoke	
	Ibuluim Kikabi	Ŋkima clan
	Miingo	Nsenene clan
	Ţebukoza	Lugave clan
	Makumbi and Ibuluim	·Ŋkima clan
Kaima	Mudjagalanyago, and Ŋkambwe	Lugave clan
Kasudju	Kabidzi ⎫ Kintu ⎰	Lugave clan
Kitunzi	Kabalu	Ndiga clan
	Misalenyoka⎫ Kyaŋgwe ⎰	Mbogoclan
	Tebakyagenda	Ndjovu clan
	Sebowa	Nsenene clan
	Kibate	Ndjovu clan
	Nyikomunyoŋga	Mamba clan
Pokino	Mukasa	Musu clan
	Magimbi	Ndjovu clan
	Mulere	Ndjovu clan
	Kasata	Mamba clan
Katambala	Ntambazi	Ndiga clan
Luwekula	Ntokota	Mamba clan
	Sebowa	Nsenene clan
	Tebakyagenda	Ndjovu clan
	Sebowa	Nsenene clan, again
	Kasáto	Mamba clan
	Nviri	Kobe clan
	Mandwambi	Lugave clan

[Mwaŋga II, Mukabya Mutesa's son] (180) married:

Wife	Father	Clan	Children
[Evairin Kulaba-ko] (Omusibika)	Nantawasa	[Ŋgabi	[Daudi Tcwa
Doisi Mwanom Bakazikubawo	Namudala	Ŋgabi]	Maliam Madzi]
Loirosa Nakibuka (Kadulubale)]	Kisomose (Katikiro)	Mamba	Naume
[Esiteri Nabunya]	Diba Omulwaza	[Fumbe]	[Yusufu Suna Kiwewa]
Samali Namu-waŋga (Sabadju)	Nyika (Kaŋgawo)	Mamba	Nasolo

Wife	Father	Clan	Children
Nabweteme	Nyika (Kaŋgawo)	Mamba	Mulindwa
Nalwoga Omu-yuŋgiriza	Kidu	Mamba	
Lakeri Mbekeka	Bindjogoli	Mamba	Ŋanda
Nakidjoba Nabulye	Katenyoleka Naŋkyama	Lugave	
Beza Batwe-gombya	Ŋgabezaya	Mpewo	.
[Damali Baita Nandjobe]	Sensalire	[Ndjovu]	[Kagolo] (killed by Kalema)
Ntoŋgo (Kabedja)	Mukasa (Kati-kiro)	Musu	
Nabisubi (Omu-waŋga)	,,	Musu	Tobi
Namirembe	Kikwata	Ŋkedje	

Mary Madzi Luwede, the daughter of Lady Doisi Mwanom Bakazikubawo, was born on the Seychelles Islands where her father was exiled by the British government. It was during his detention on these islands that Mwaŋga was converted and baptised with the Christian name of Daniel.

Mwaŋga also married approximately two hundred reserve wives. In addition he had some women who belonged to his grandfather, making a total of about seven hundred. He also had about one thousand five hundred maiden servants.

Mwaŋga became king in October 1884. He founded his capital at Meŋgo hill and named his palace Mukulu atamakage. This means literally "The chief destroys his own home." Actually it means that the chief who does right uplifts his home, but he who does wrong destroys it. He himself was a bad king and brought on his own ruin. He named his twin Walugya after that of Mwaŋga I.

Mutesa's body lay in state for five days before it was buried. Mwaŋga was enthroned on the day of the burial. He was well liked by the people. He was fond of young people and had not enough respect for the chiefs. He was very handsome, with rounded eyes and a beard of extraordinary quality.

These were the chiefs who comprised his government:

Prime Minister	Mukasa	Musu clan
Kimbugwe	Nyikomunyoŋga	Mamba clan
Kago	Kanabi	Musu clan

Mukwenda	Nuwa Kabuŋga	Mbogo clan
Sekibobo	Mukasa	Musu clan, — he was also prime minister.
Kaŋgawo	Kibiraŋgo	Lugave clan, — he was succeeded by Yusufu Waswa
Mugema	Makumbi and Ibulaim Kikabi	Ŋkima clan
Kaima	Kagyo and Lukómwa	Fumbe clan
Kasudju	Kabidzi and his son Kadzi	Lugave clan
Kitunzi	Muguluma	Ndjovu clan
	Adoloniko Kamya	Ndiga clan
Pokino	Magimbi Kamanyiro and Tebukoza	Lugave clan
Katambala	Ntambazi, Kinobe and Bira	Ndiga clan
Luwekula	Male	Kobe clan
	Kinobe	Ndiga clan

Mwaŋga was dethroned because of the hostility of the so-called Christians. When he returned to the throne he made the following appointments:

Prime Minister	Apolo Kagwa	Nsenene clan
Kimbugwe	Kigula	Mamba clan
	He was followed by	
	Stanisirasi Mugwanya	Butiko clan
	Nikodem Sebwato	Mamba clan
	Semei Kakuŋgulu	

After the resignation of Kakuŋgulu the office remained vacant.

Kago	Matayo Nsubuga and Paulo Nsubuga Ba-kuŋga	Mamba clan
	Yakobo Lule Musadja-lumbwa	Mpewo clan
Mukwenda	Yona Waswa	Fumbe clan
	Paulo Nsubuga	Mamba clan
Sekibobo	Alikisi Sebowa	Fumbe clan
	Paulo Nsubuga, Niko-dem Sebwato, Misu-sera Kibude	Mamba clan

Kaŋgawo	Yozefu Kiwanuka	Butiko clan
	Zakaliya Kizito Kisiŋ-giri	Mamba clan
Mugema	Djoswa Kate Damulira	Ŋkima clan
Kaima	Kityo	Mamba clan
	Tomasi Semukasa	Mutima clan
	Danyeri Sematimba	Ŋoŋge clan
Kasudju	Lulika and Asanti Se-mindi	Lugave clan
Kitunzi	Adolonika Kamya Paulo Nsubuga Sitefano Kalibwane Samwiri Mukasa	Mamba clan
	Yokana Muwaŋga	Kobe clan
Pokino	Nikodem Sebwato Alikisi Sebowa	Fumbe clan
Katambala	Lawi Sekiti and Bira II	Ndiga clan
	Taibu Magato	Musu clan
Luwekula	Dembo	Kobe clan
	Sedulaka Kiuli	Ndiga clan
	Sepiriya Mutagwanya	Ŋgabi clan

[Kiwewa, son of Mutesa, married the following women:] (180)

Wife	Father	Clan	Children
Sabadju	Kanyandjwe	[Ŋoŋge	
[Alirwa	Ndalike	,,	[Hana Madzi
Lwandeta	Lule	,,	Namika, Mususi
Kadja	Sebowa	Nsenene	Kibuka
Butema]	Ntale (Muima)	Ŋkima]	Simbwa]
Mbagumide (Kabedja)	Gundju	Butiko	
Bukirwa (Nasaza)	Nsamba	Ŋgabi	
[Tebalyoyerwa (Omulinda-madzi)]	Nsamba	,,	Agati Kagere Tcwa, Gendza
[Nambi	Katenda	[,,	[Muwaŋga
Bwaŋgu	Sebidjerwe	,,	
Lozaliya	Sabadu	,,	Nabada
Nambi II	Gabuŋga	Mamba	Sekamanya
Namubiru	Gabuŋga	Mamba	Augusitini Teban-deke
Nambadjwe	Gabuŋga		Gulubagwira
Nambi III]	Katenda	Mamba]	Namulinzi]

Wife	Father	Clan	Children
Teyansigira	Katenda	Mamba	Namulinzi
Zandaba	Mugula	Lugave	Nasiwa, Nasuswa
Namusoke (Kadulubale)	Kidandala	Nvuma	Lukoŋgwa, Kiwanuka, Walulyo
Namuli Omufumbiro	Bulezi	Mpindi .	Lulaba, Kagumya
Luleba (Omusenero)	Gadimiba	Lugave	Muinda

[Kiwewa was enthroned as king on August 2nd, 1888, but he reigned for only seventy-two days.] (229) Then he was captured by order of Kalema and put to death. This was done in most inhuman fashion. He was locked up for seven days without a drop of water or a bite to eat, and was then shot to death. His body was burned up in the cell, together with those of his brothers and his children. About thirty people were burned then. He was buried at Masanafu hill. Kiwewa was fond of old people but he was also a friend of drunkards.

These were the chiefs who helped him during his brief reign:

Prime Minister	Henery Nyonyintono	Ndiga clan, who was also Sekibobo
Kimbugwe	Bukulu	Fumbe clan
Kago	Sulumani Basereka	Nsenene clan
Mukwenda	Apolo Kagwa Kalibala and Tefiro Kulugi	Nsenene clan Ngeye clan
Kaŋgawo	Kapalaga	Nyonyi clan
Mugema	Ibulaim Kikabi who was replaced by	Ŋkima clan
	Yahaya Sekyeru	Ŋkima clan
Kaima	Lukomwa	Fumbe clan
Kitunzi	Adolonika Kamya	Ndiga clan
Pokino	Muguluma	Ndjovu clan
Katambala	Bira	Ndiga clan

Kalema, son of Mutesa, married:

Wife	Father	Clan	Children
[Zezefina Nampa Nakibuka,	Bakabulindi	[Ŋgeye	[Ndaula Alamazane
Nabiboge]	Kibaya	Nsenene]	Zozefu, Musandje,] Walugembe

Wife	Father	Clan	Children
Sofi Kabaka-longosa	Kinyoro	Ŋkima	[Besemensi, Hana Dimbwe
[Nabikukuzi	Djumba	[Ŋkima	Zimbwe]
Veneneka Nabi-wemba]	Wakoli Musoga	Ŋgabi]	Yuniya,] Maliya, [Kamuwanda,], Lubuga
Ndjera Sabadu	Gabuŋga	[Mamba] (180)	

[He was enthroned on October 2. and immediately was circumcised and became a Mohammedan.] (279) His reign was short. Because of disturbing internal wars he did not name his house. [He was deposed in October 1889, and fled to Bunyoro, where he died of plague. He was buried at Mende.

He is said to have been fond of women and might have grown to have a reputation like Suna "speaking through his wives who were dear to him."] (230)

Both Kiwewa and Kalema made very few official marriages, having merely those they had married as princes and some of Mwaŋgas'. This was due to the skirmishes which constantly threatened their lives.

These are some of his chiefs:

Prime Minister	Muguluma	Ndjovu clan
Kimbugwe	Kikwalo	Mpindi clan
Kago	Yusufu Waswa	Lugave clan
Kaŋgawo	Sempa	Ŋkima clan
Kaima	Koŋgo	Ndjovu clan
Mugema	Yahaya Sekyeru	Ŋkima clan
Pokino	Muguluma	Ndjovu clan
Katambala	Bira	Ndiga clan

On October 5th, 1889, [Mwaŋga was reenthroned. The country was peaceful for a time. In January 1892 he fought against the British and lost. He fled] (230) to Kiziba and remained there for two months, and then he returned to the throne once more. He became disgusted with the country and abdicated in 1897. He was bitter against the English and worked on several plans against them, but they all came to nought. When he gave up the throne he went to Budu and refused to leave despite the invitations to return he received from all his chiefs. In July he went to German East Africa whence the government transferred him to Mwanza.

[Daudi Tcwa, the son of Mwaŋga, became king on August 12th, 1897. He was just one year and six months old at the time.] (230)

During the four months when Apolo Kagwa was in Basoga fighting against the Banubi, Mwaŋga escaped from Mwanza and came to Kyaka village, where he induced several warriors to join him. He fought his way to Bunyoro and crossed the Tcope river into Bukedi, where he joined Kabalega, King of Bunyoro. After about a year they were captured by the British. [The Kings were both sent to the Seychelles Islands as rebels. Mwaŋga died there] (230) in 1903. He is said to have peen converted and baptized before his death. He was buried on the Seychelles Island. His wife Doisi Mwanom supplied this information about his death. She returned to Buganda in the company of Yusufu Mwandjale, Petero Yona Balizakiwa: Maliya Mwandjale, Maliam Madzi Luwede, and the two children of Mwandjale.

The officials of Buganda requested of the British that they return the remains of Mwaŋga. This request was finally granted. Mika Sematimba and Petero Yona Balizakiwa were officially commissioned to go for the body. On August 3rd, 1910, it was buried at Kasubi in the tomb occupied by Mutesa.

The body was met at the port by a specially appointed committee of eminent men, and five hundred others to carry it. The party arrived at Meŋgo about twelve o'clock and the body was placed beside the house of Kisiŋgiri... That afternoon there was a church ceremony..

That night two of the regents and many of the chiefs remained in the palace for the "king's consolation" according to the traditional custom. In the morning the prime minister informed the king that he would be sent for at nine o'clock. Then the king with several chiefs and a crowd of people went to Kasubi. The coffin was opened and the body viewed and identified.

The body was buried in a tomb of brick and cement. It was in a triple coffin of wood and steel, wrapped with many yards of cloth. After this, the king and his brothers went to Muzib(u)-Azala-Mpaŋga. The Kasudju took the king by the hand and gave him over to the prime minister, saying, "Here is your king." The tomb was then closed up with bricks. That concluded the funeral ceremonies...

The next morning Kibale, Mpewo clan, and Nakatanza, Lugave clan, came to the palace and knocked at the door of the king's house. At eight o'clock a council was held by the provincial chiefs to lay plans for the enthronement. Mugema, who tied the knot in the king's bark cloth on the right shoulder, demanded the right to tie the one on the left shoulder. This caused a disagreement in the council. It was finally settled against Mugema by the men of the royal family. Then the chiefs went to the royal palace.

Kabumba, of the Lugave clan, brought the carpet and Kiini, of the Mamba clan, the tanner, brought the skins of lions, leopards, hyenas, and cows. Apolo Kagwa escorted the king and his sister, Djuma Katebe. He headed the procession, carrying the king's spears and shields. He marched at the right of the king because he is next to the king and insures his peace. At the palace gate Mugema led the king to the throne and placed him on it. He then placed the barkcloth on the king and knotted it on the right shoulder, as an indication that the king was the owner of the country. He laid a calfskin over the barkcloth because Kimera wore a calfskin. Then he said, "You will perform all the acts and duties befitting a king."

The Kasudju knotted a barkcloth on the king's left shoulder which meant, "You are His Majesty who rules over all other officials and men." On top of this he put a leopard skin meaning, "A king is the leopard; the common people are squirrels." Then he too said, "You will perform all the acts and duties befitting a king."

Kakinda, of the Kobe clan, brought a differently decorated barkcloth and this was placed over all the other ceremonial robes. This was several yards long and was wrapped from the right shoulder around the body and back again.

Then the Mukwenda, Sabagabo, brought a shield and two spears and handed them to the king. This meant that the king would overthrow his enemies. Kadjubi tied a string of sparkling beads about the king's left arm as a memorial to Wanyana, saying, "You are Kimera." Segulu, of the Lugave clan, put a bracelet on the king's right hand to show that he among the princes was the king elect. Namutwe, assistant Sekibobo, handed a bow and arrow to the king to assure him of his jurisdiction over the subjugated Basagala. Those who remember Greek history know that there was a king who had a slave remind him about his victory over the Athenians at all his meals (sic!).

Kaima by virtue of his office of chief in charge of the weapons brought a bow and arrow to the king. Then Masembe came and stood before the king with a milk jar. Mugema introduced him, saying, "This is your head herdsman who takes care of Namala's cow from which your great-great-grandfather, Kimera, drank his milk." Then the king touched the jar and Masembe took it away. Sebalidja, the head shepherd, brought a brass milk jar, and handed it to Mpiŋga, who had been Kimera's shepherd. Mpiŋga introduced him to the king, saying, "When milking my cow Mbulide, given me by Kimera, I use this jar."

Luboyera, of the Butiko clan, brought a beer jar known as Mwendanvuma, saying "This is the jar in which I make your beer." Kalinda presented the type of jar in which the king's drinking water is kept, saying, "This is your water jar."

Semwaŋga and Kabogoza, Ŋoŋge clan, the barkcloth makers, brought a mallet, saying, "This is the mallet upon which your barkcloths are made." Segirinya, Ŋgo clan, brought the iron tool used in engraving the crown and royal stick. He presented this to the king, saying, "This is omuindu[1]. I use it to adorn your crown and to fashion your walking sticks." Walukaga, of the Kasimba clan, a blacksmith, brought a hammer, saying, "With this I make the spear with which you conquer." Mutalaga, of the Nvuma clan, another blacksmith, brought a dagger. He gave it to Kasudju, who gave it to the king saying, "Whoever rebels against you, you will destroy with this dagger."

Then Mugema introduced the chief royal drums, known as Mudjaguzo. Kaula, of the Lugave clan, brought the drum sticks and Kasudju gave them to the king. The king beat the drum. Kimomera, of the Butiko clan, the assistant drummer, gave the king another pair of drumsticks and the king beat on another drum known as Namanyonyi.

Muyandja, of the Nyonyi clan, brought an axe and said, "This is your axe Naŋkuŋga that builds your boats." Omusoloza[2], of the Nyonyi clan, presented the king with two pieces of firewood, and said, "These two pieces of wood keep the fire in Gombolola, whence you obtain the ashes to smear yourself for war."

This ended the introductory ceremony. Several others followed.

Sekaiba, of the Mbogo clan, came covered with a barkcloth known as "Throne" and carried the king on his shoulders for about twenty feet, while the princesses and the huge crowd that had assembled paid homage to the enthroned king. They shouted and gave the yells of their clans. Then the prime minister with a shield and two spears escorted the king to his dwelling house. Here the relatives of the king offered him gifts. They came in order, his grandfather, then his aunts, his sisters, brothers and the other princes. They were required to stand at the end of the carpet and introduce themselves formally.

After that another group of kinsmen came. This comprised the children of the princesses. They adorned their heads in the proper fashion and came singing beautiful melodies. The king gave them a bull and bade them farewell. His mother's relatives also offered gifts, and introduced themselves. Before the conclusion of the

---

[1] a stick with branches.   [2] tax-collector.

5

ceremony his grandfathers of the Ɖoŋge clan, the grandfathers of Tcwa I of the Ɖgeye clan, and those of Kimera of the Nsenene clan, in the order named, introduced themselves.

These are the chiefs holding office at the time of writing:

Prime Minister	Apolo Kagwa	Nsenene clan
	Stanisirasi Mugwanya	Butiko clan was also appointed, as a representative of the Catholic faction in the country
Kaŋgawo	Zakaliya Kizito	Mamba clan

These three were appointed regents to carry on the government during the youth of Daudi. When he took the throne they retained the three positions of most importance created by the Uganda Agreement. They became, respectively, head of the Parliament, head of the Department of Justice, and head of the treasury.

Kago	Yakobo Lule Musadjalumbwa	Mpewo clan
Mukwenda	Paulo Nsubuga Bakuŋga	Mamba clan
Sekibobo	Misusera Kibude.	Mamba clan
	He was succeeded by	
	Ham Mukasa	Ndjovu clan
Kaŋgawo	Samwiri Mukasa Ganafa	Nsenene clan
Mugema	Djoswa Kate Damulira	Ɖkima clan
Kaima	Matayo Kisule,	Ɖgeye clan
	followed by	
	Andereya Kiwanuka	Mbogo clan
	Semeo Nsubuga	
Kasudju	Asanti Semindi	Lugave clan
Kitunzi	Yokana Muwaŋga	Kobe clan
Pokino	Alikisi Sebowa	Fumbe clan
Kamuswaga	Edwadi Kezekiya Ndaula,	Ɖgabi clan
	then	
	Sifasi Djodje Kabumbuli	

The men who served the various chiefs on their estates were mostly young men. It was they who were the most energetic and successful in the looting campaigns the king ordered from time to time against the neighbors. When the booty was brought home the chief selected that which pleased him most from among the loot of his subordinates, and so became a rich man. The king might show favoritism and assign his favorite chiefs to frequent and lucrative campaigns.

This custom may have had something to do with the Baganda ignorance of trading. They were used to use force to get anything

they desired, or else to receive it from the king as a gift. Those who
were appointed to the various estates cultivated them by means of
the peasants, who moved wherever they pleased. They very com-
monly went to the estate of a newly appointed chief who they
thought might be honored with presents and booty. This meant that
there was very great instability, the great mass of the peasantry
shifting about and chiefs long established being left alone with
their wealth.

CHAPTER VIII.

MARRIAGE OF THE KING.

There were two forms of marriage possible for the king. In the
first the chiefs and landlords throughout the country held marriage
councils, selected virgin girls from twelve to seventeen, and presented the comeliest of these to the king. The other form was [by
the selection on the part of the king himself among girls sent to
the palace.........] (87)

[Despite the large number of wives at the palace, the control over
them was effective in preventing disturbances and jealousy.] (81)
Those wives of whom the king was fondest were given superior
positions of supervision. Their parents were also honored with
presents and appointments to minor posts.

Girls who were sent to the palace and whom the king had not
actually married nor appointed to any regular position were the
group from whom he selected wives..... If the king wished to give
maiden servants to his wives he ordered a chief to go out among the
peasants and select the best-looking girls. Women captured in war
also served as maiden servants in the palace. The king divided them
among his favorite wives and their immediate subordinates so
that these might maintain their positions of dignity.

Servitude of this sort was practically slavery. It was practised
by all the people of rank. When a chief gave a man servant of his a
woman to marry, the children of the pair became his servants too.

Closely related to this is the custom whereby the sisters and
brothers of a married woman, and other close relatives, had the
right to take her children to work in their households, and the
father could avoid this only by exchanging goods for them. They
returned to their parents when they were grown up. If there were
several children not all of them might be saved from being brought
up by their aunts and uncles.

The custom of marrying several wives is a relatively recent one.
Formerly the king married only one wife, Kadulubale, who was
responsible for the care of the entire palace. Later on two more

5*

wives, Kabedja and Nasaza were added. Kabedja took over charge of half the palace. [Nasaza was the custodian of the hair and fingernail clippings of the king, which she kept until the death of the king and then took to be buried with the body.] (84)

When the system of plural marriage became established, the queen always outranked the other wives, and Kabedja and Nasaza were immediately below her. The chiefs in their homes also had ranking wives, called by the same titles. It was not till the reign of Katerega that polygamy became popular, and the common people began to marry two or three wives apiece. Katerega and his chiefs decided to demand of the prominent and wealthy chiefs taxes in the form of goods, to be given to the wives of the king. This custom was not abolished until the reign of Mwaŋga.

The following classification indicates the way in which the different chiefs paid their taxes to the kings' wives.

Wife	Chief
Kadulubale	Kaŋgawo, Muwemba, Mulamba, Omutete, Sabakaki
Kabedja	Mukwenda, Sekibobo, Omukomazi, Serugo, Nampagi, Lugumba, Mukusu, Kibale, Nakatanza, Lubobi, Kaula, Omusoloza
Nasaza	Kasudju, Miro, Sabaganzi
Nanzigu	Katikiro, Djumba, Namuyimba I and II, Kasumba, Natigo, Omusamba, Katanda, Kabi
Kikome	Kitunzi, Bitaŋga
Luiga	Kakembo
Nakadu	Pokino
Sabadu	Kago, Wakoli, Sekyoya
Omukabya	Mukabya
Owekatikam	Namutwe
Omukebezi	Mukebezi
Omwaŋga	Mwaŋga
Muwunda	Katambala, Nuŋga, Katenda, Luimbazi, Kadjerero
Omwaziza	Mwaziza
Nakasala	Kauta, Banda Omubumbi, Sedagala
Omuwaŋga	Senkezi, Bidjugo, Mulyabyaki, Mazige, Namuguzi, Walukaga
Nakidjoba	Myamba
Omusuna	Musuna
Omunakulya	Munakulya
Omukwanya	Mukwanya
Omuterega	Muterega
Omugoloba	Mugoloba

Omulaula	Mulaula
Nakimera	Kinyoro, Kamuswaga, Gwobalira, Mpandju, and Nsambya
Omubiŋge	Mubiŋge
Naŋkole	Seŋkole
Omuwewesi	Mukweya
Omumanya	Mumanya
Omusaka	Barkclothmakers
Omuwaŋguzi	Muwaŋguzi
Omunywa	Munywa
Omulaŋgira	Mulaŋgira
Omusenero	Seruti
Omutesa	Mutesa
Omukambata	Mukambata
Omusigula	Musigula
Omukeira	Mukera
Omuwambya	Muwambya
Nagai	Kaima
Nabanaku	Nsandja
	Diviners
Omukwakula	Mukwakula
Solamumi	Omugoma, player of drum
	Nakawaŋguzi

CHAPTER X

NABIKANDE AND BAYOMBA

[Nabikande] and Bayomba, [the sisters of the queen mother, were the midwives for the wives of the king...] (50)...

[Nabikande took the pregnant queen to a new home which was built especially for her. No one else was permitted to stay there. Everything she was to use — clothes, bedding, utensils — was new. Her maid servants were expected to obey the restrictions, and never dine with other people. Should they want to eat while in the gardens they baked their meals and ate alone.] (51)

There was a custom of cutting a bunch of fruit off a plantain tree which was known as "to steal." It was done very secretly and therefore symbolized the strict confinement in which the woman was kept. All her movements were supervised. Until she gave birth a servant stood at her back whenever the medicine for the protection of the expected child was served. [This was known as "The prisoner's guard."] (51)

When the child was born the maid servants went down to [cut a bunch of bananas to indicate the sex of the child born. Should it be a girl one from the left was cut, for a boy one from the right.](52) The tree was carefully trimmed so that those watching might know.

[Nabikande then entered the house and asked the woman what her clan was, so that the ceremonial feast might be given.] (52) If the child died during the cremony the mother might return to the palace that same day.

When the baby was two months old the king went to the house of Nabikande, where the baby was nursed, to visit it. After seven months the mother was allowed to visit the king, at the house known as Nakabunda, in the palace. As a sign that she was the mother of an unweaned baby she wore strands of flax-like grass about her neck.

There were some associated superstitions. If a woman was acting demoniacally she was believed to have been caught by a demon which was trying to destroy the baby. The attendants therefore forced a poor peasant woman nursing her baby to give her child into the care of the maiden servants and nurse that of the queen. Her baby was fed milk and she never saw it until it was grown. She was required to keep the baby of the king in good condition (Roscoe says this was done when the king wished to keep the wife at the palace.) (53)

When the time came to wean the child the king went to Nabikande's home where a great feast was prepared. The baby was then returned to the mother from whom it had been separated for fear of the demon. Then the king returned to the palace and sent to Nabikande things to distribute among the wives who had attended the feast. The next morning the midwives shaved these women behind their ears both as an adornment and a sign that they had borne children to the king.

In the evening a "king's babies' reception" was held. The king received and acknowledged his babies at the home of Kadulubale. The wives were divided into two groups, those with baby boys to the right and those with baby girls to the left. The king stood in the doorway and demanded "Give me my children". The first born boy was brought to him to be touched. Then Nabikande and Bayomba introduced all the children and their mothers. (Roscoe has this done by Kiwewa immediately after the weaning.) The children were touched by the king and then returned to their mothers. This was the "Royal Nursing". All the princes were nursed and then all the princesses. The first of the princes was known as Kiwewa, and the first of the princesses as Nasolo.

Then the king, the children, and their mothers, went to a house called Makumbi, where the girls were taken through but the boys around the house.

The ceremony of naming the children was next. The Kago killed a goat and gave the liver to the queen to bake. The king then cut it into pieces and gave one to each of the children and each of the mothers, taking one himself and giving one to the Kago. Then Kasudju spread a barkcloth on the verandah and all the children and their mothers came and sat on it. The king stood in the doorway, and Kasudju told him a name for each of the children, beginning with the oldest prince. When all the children had had these names given them by the king, the chiefs left the king alone among his wives. He then jumped over the mother of the first son, and this woman jumped over all the others.

The next morning the queen made a feast for all the wives, using the goat of which the liver had been used. All the remains were burnt to ashes, for it was unlawful for anyone else to use that meat. Then the wives took the children back to Mubisi, brother of the queen mother, shaved their heads, and returned to the palace. The queen shaved the mothers of sons, and Kabadja the mothers of daughters. After this ceremony the mothers returned to their former positions in the palace with their own children.

It is now thought that the objections raised to the nursing of their own children by some women were due to the endeavors of diviners to maintain their positions of prestige.

After the children had remained in the palace for some time the king sent them to be brought up by some of the prominent chiefs... When they grew to be ten years old [he gave each of them an estate and servants.] (73).........

The other sisters of the queen mother, Wanyana, Mubisi, Nakaberenge and Danda, acted as assistant midwives. Danda was midwife to the wives of the brothers of the king, who were known as the "little fathers". This was a precaution against the possible growth of power of the brothers or their children. As soon as a son was born to one of them at the house of Danda it was choked to death.... The children of the sons of the reigning king were not put to death.... If the sons of a king obtained control of the kingdom when their father died, his brothers who were still alive were no longer eligible and so when their wives were pregnant they did not need to be guarded nor their babies choked. These surviving princes were looked up to with respect by the young king.........

[To assure the king a long and peaceful reign, Mondo, Mulere, Nakasese, and Namutala formed a corps of spies who went about the country. If they heard any one speaking against the king, the royal household, or the kingdom, they reported him] (20) to the queen mother (Roscoe says to the prime minister) who reported him to the king. The king decided upon the punishment to be meted out to him. The property of a rich chief might be confiscated, or his office taken from him..........

CHAPTER XI.

THE KING'S PALACE.

This description gives the names of the more important houses but merely mentions those of lesser importance.

[In the royal court was the court house] (260) Gombolola. [Here the prime minister presided.] The word means "to disentangle", because those who were tangled up in all sorts of disputes here came to settle them and those who failed to pay debts brought their grievances there. [The word of the prime minister was in many cases final. Sometimes there was appeal to the king.] (235) During the reign of Mutesa, the prime minister, leaving an associate behind him there, was promoted to another court house within the palace which was known as Maseŋgeregansanze.

[Gombolola was situated outside the palace but within the boundaries of the royal grounds.] (258) [At the right of the palace gateway, Waŋkaki, was a royal furnace] (202) called Gombolola. This too was a court house, for the settlement of problems and disputes arising among the men who were in charge of gathering wood for the royal fireplaces. Part was used for drying the wood....

(Most of the following material agrees fairly well with the plan of the royal enclosure, and the plan of the capital, in the appendix to Roscoe. I include here merely the scattered additional notes which were to be found in this material. Ed.) (In the following description the palace of Mutesa has been used as an example. E. B. K.)

Makumbi was the building in which the king fulfilled various ceremonial obligations. It was behind Muzibu-azala-mpaŋga.

Bawanika was a gateway leading into the hall called Ndogo-bukaba. This was on the left as one entered the grounds. Here the Royal Drums were kept. [Roscoe says they were kept in Batenga.)

When the king himself appeared in court the persons who lost the cases then on trial were very seriously illtreated. They were bound from head to toe by long ropes suspended from some distance away and were pulled over the ground. The name given the court house — Maseŋgere-gansanze — means "I have been met by ores" which are sharper than merely the earth. The reference is to the severity of the bruises sustained by the victim.

Ndimunyoro-sirimuganda, in the courtyard of Bulaŋge, the council house, was the place in which all sorts of drinks for the king were kept. (Roscoe says the king's bathtub was here.) The other house here was for those who carried the king's chair.

There were five different gateways in the courtyard leading to different important houses.

Wakoli, entrance to and from the houses of parliament.

Another to the house where the treasure was kept.

One to the cooking department.

One to the courthouse.

One to the dwelling house of the king, which was difficult of access.

From the main entrance one passed into Bamozera alley (named after the people loved by the king) whence gateways led into the small ivory hall owned by Lady Luiga. From this three communicating doorways led to [the dwelling house, Twekobe.] In its front courtyard was a small hall occupied by the wives who tie the calves and attend to the beer. On the left, facing the king's house, was a small house for the beer maker and her assistants, the Abakebezi or Abanywa. Here the king remained long and made frequent calls.

[Behind the king's dwelling was a house, Kalyakoka, for the private use of the king.] It was tended by members of the Musu clan. [Opposite it was a cottage called Bisera, for the lady in attendance, the Omukokiro.

[Another house in the front courtyard was called Bumenya,[1] "Even a strong man bows down to love affairs." Here the women, presided over by Omunywa, held meetings. Behind it were three houses: Balimwagula[2], "If you visit the king while he is angry you are likely to be killed" owned by Omudjuna; (Roscoe says it was here that wives waited to be called to the royal couch.) Bweserandabate-bumalamanda[3], "Do not hesitate to advise yourself", owned by Omusuna; and Kitente, a house after the Kisoga fashion, owned by Omuwalula.

Ŋkwana-bukopi[4] was just outside the courtyard of Bumenya. The name means "One who finds favor with the king is no longer a peasant and does not like to be regarded as such." This belonged to the ladies-in-waiting, who were chosen for special service because of their appearance. (This was another house where wives waited.)

[1] lit., it breaks. [2] lit., they will scratch him.
[3] lit., the boiling millet which is seen does not waste charcoal.
[4] lit., I make friends with the peasantry.

The kitchen was in Kalyomu (Roscoe says Kagango) near Katikam road. Nakasala headed the department. There were three other houses, in one of which Namunyoro inspected the food that was to be distributed.

[There were four small houses near Namutide road, Namutide, Ndeba, Nakabunda and another.] They were owned by Lady Mukomweidzi. [Nakabunda was the king's reception hall. Here came the wives who were staying at Nabikande's. Kimbugwe occupied a house near the small public hall but the twins were kept in Nakabunda.

The following are the main entrances to the palace:

> [Waŋkaki, the main gateway]. Kept by Mulamba, the head doorkeeper.
>
> [Naloŋgo,] also important. Kept by Sabawali, an assistant doorkeeper.
>
> [Lubaŋga]. Under the care of Omusale[1] of Kigazi. Omusale of Kigalagala helped.
>
> [Sabavuma] was important. Its doorkeeper was named after it.
>
> [Wansanso]. Under the management of Sabagabo. Sabagabo of Kigalagala also resided here.
>
> [Kagerekam]. This name means a single foot. It was a private entrance and no one was allowed to enter unless accompanying the king.
>
> [Kagerekam]. Under the care of the head butler. All beer and other drinks for the king were brought in here.
>
> Wakoli. Under the care of the doorkeeper Sabadu and also Sabadu of Kigalagala. It was used mostly by ladies coming as messengers to the king from his mother.
>
> [Naloŋgo]. Under the care of less important officers.

As a rule the palace was built so as to face the east, as that is the direction whence the ancestors of the kings were supposed to have come. It is for the same reason that the kings were buried at Busiro. It was meant merely as a sign of respect.

[The palace was an oval enclosure about 1105 by 1122 yards] (200) by European measure. The native measure was the fathom. In assigning work, each county was assigned the space measured by fifty of these.

In alleys about the halls Nsigo and Kandogobukaba and in the front yard of Maseŋgere (there were camps set up with skin tents for the king's bodyguard.) (201) The less important servants had their camp on Namutide road, and on the back porch of the house

---

[1] assistant war leader.

of parliament. Some young boys were lodged in the king's house.
The king's treasurer also had rooms there for himself and his
servants.

Sabakaki, the king's head servant, had quarters in Saŋga, which
had at one time been for the use of the king's wives. Some of the
important servants stayed there with him, but most of them merely
camped in the streets. Their chief job was to bring in firewood for
the torch which accompanied the king on all his visits.

Outside the palace proper were the quarters of cabinet and parliament members, some of the wives of the king, and various temples
(sabo). (R. Appendix; Plan of capitol)..........

In the palace of Lady Kabedja there were eighteen houses, among
them Kinauataka and Babindjayeko. There were two halls, Naki-
buka and Yesibika, in which Nantaba, a horn, was lodged. In this
palace the king put the skins on his drums Mudjaguzo, Nakawaŋguzi,
Mulyabyaki, and Nadjemba.

In Nakimera's palace there were only four houses.

There were six houses in Nambowoze's palace.

Nanzigu's had twenty-one houses. In one of these the horn known
as Mpeta was kept.

Kimbugwe's palace was divided into two parts, one side with
twenty-five houses for the twin, and the other with fifty for his
own use. Among the houses for the twin were Nakatuza and Kiza-
nyira. The twins occupied very magnificent beds. It is said that the
twins of Mutesa still occupies its bed. Some of the twins were here
instead of in Busiro county, and their queens took as much pride
in their duties as though they were caring for a living king.

[When a chief was appointed to build a house for the king, he had
to purchase the crown] (246) at the price of two women and two
goats. The middle crown cost him a woman, a cow, and a goat, and
the third a cow and a goat. These expenses all had to be met by the
chief appointed. The strain was sometimes so great that lesser
chiefs failed and lost their positions, becoming servants to the king
or taking minor posts under other chiefs.

[About the palace of the king were groups of houses belonging to
various chiefs........]

[From the road to Nabikande to the house of the chief of police
(next to Nakulabye road)] were the quarters of the butlers.

The palace of the Katikiro had over a hundred houses in it. They
were arranged on four main thoroughfares. Kago, Mukwenda,
Sekibobo, Kaŋgawo, Mugema, Pokino, Kitunzi, Katambala,
Kasudju, and Kaima, all had many buildings in their quarters, the
number varying with the number of wives to be accomodated.

ARCHITECTURE.

The following is the plan of construction of the house of a chief:
First several different sorts of trees and reeds had to be cut:
Pillars were set up. (These were trees with the branches but not the
bark removed, though occasionally they might be stripped and then
grass-decorated. They were about twelve feet high for the four
centre ones, set in a square, and a trifle less for the semicircle of
eight to twelve poles. Heavy ones about a foot in diameter were
used.) There were also supporting pillars — (These were set up
diagonally, sloping from a point immediately outside the other
circle up to a point midway on the wall or roof. All were set into the
ground.) Seaweed was also cut, (and a fibrous and pithy reed, which
was dried and the bark split off for use.)

Then the architect was notified to come. He gave orders to begin
the proceeding traditionally known as the "shooting of the house".
A mat was made by interweaving in simple checker pattern the
reeds which had been prepared, till a small flat section was formed.
This was then set at the top of the house over the frame-work of
the four center poles, and the work went on downwards. (The
workers reached the roof by means of a scaffolding set up about
the poles. Sometimes the roofing was sharply peaked instead of
flat at the top. The crown was a ring at the top of the frame).
The work might be greatly simplified by setting long reeds from
the centre of the top to the ground and them weaving upon these
as a basis, but this was done only by the peasants. The inside of
the house was then levelled, and the supporting poles adjusted so
that the weight of the roofing was borne by them. Then the porch
was built. (This was a rectangular extension in front of the roofing,
beyond the doorway. It had a rounded roof, and the thatching here
was lighter than that of the house proper. There was also an un-
walled part known as the verandah.)

The next stage in the building of the house was the thatching.
Then the inside was arranged. The fireplace was in the center. The
doorway was decorated. Fences were built to assure privacy and
dignity.

The houses of the peasants were on the same plan but were not so
well or strongly built. (The houses themselves when well built
lasted five years or more, but they usually needed re-thatching.)

Today there is considerable modification of the house form, as
people are anxious to have doors with locks on their houses.

(The notes here in parentheses are from information supplied
by E. B. Kalibala.-Ed.)

CHAPTER XII.

THE KING'S PARLIAMENT.

[On the day that parliament was to assemble the prime minister went to the king. His drum was beaten as an announcement to the public.] (258) He went directly to Maseŋgeregansanze where the other chiefs joined him. Sometimes the assembling took place in Ndogobukaba. (R. says the audiences were held in Bulaŋge.) (258)

[The king would send one of his messengers to the minister to inquire as to what members were present.] He would kneel down and say, "The king sent me to see you," and the prime minister would reply, "Has he conquered ?", to which the messenger would respond, "He has conquered." Then he would explain his mission and the prime minister would say, "Yes, they are all present." Then the chiefs introduced themselves, Kimbugwe first, and then the county chiefs in the order of their rank..... Then the assistant county chiefs would introduce themselves, and then the petty chiefs. Each gave his rank and his private name. To each the king's representative replied, "I have seen you." The messengers were so trained as to remember all these people no matter how many there were.

After all had finished the messenger would announce, "I whom the king sent am gone." The whole house would reply. "He has conquered." Then he would return to the king and kneeling submissively would say, "The prime minister has acknowledged the message and sent me to see you." — "Yes," said the king. Then the messenger would proceed to introduce all the chiefs with their names, but when he had named two-thirds of them he would stop, and finish by saying, "All Buganda is present."

[When the king was to appear before Parliament] he wore his royal robes and went either to Maseŋgeregansanze or to [Bulaŋge.] He invited some of the more important chiefs to a private council. Then the others came to the door and announced themselves in formal terms. "I, Omutabuza, (who does not inquire) have come to see the married man." — "He has heard, the strength which breaks an axe to render it unrepairable" would be the answer, or "I have come to see the owner." — "The married man has heard you." When about ten have done this the king has them admitted, and they knelt in a group before the king. "All is well," they said. "All is well at Busiro," the others answered. Then they were all seated.

In this way the king was able to become familiar with a number of his chiefs. However, those who were not in this number had no way of becoming known to the chief. It was not possible for one of no rank to introduce himself to the king.

[At some meetings the representatives of the king did the introducing.] (259) He led them all into the presence of the king. The prime minister then knelt, saying "You have conquered." The king said "Yes," and all the chiefs, keeping their seats, answered in unison.

When Mutesa became a Mohammedan and learned to read he refused to have homage done him in this fashion. He ordered that he be greeted only with the Swahili word, "Sibwakeri". When he was not well, he was greeted with, "Is all well?" When the king was confined to the house, introducing of the members of the council was omitted, and instead the king had only private conferences with the important men. Sometimes he admitted all the council that they might see that there was nothing seriously wrong with him. Mwaŋga retained this system.

The representatives were trained from childhood by their parents. They were made familiar with the procedure, and with the traditions, including the names of the kings, their wives, chiefs and so forth. The father would cut a number of pegs, and name each after some important historical personage. Then before his sons he would call out the name represented by each, expecting them then to be able to tell him what any one stood for. Thus it was possible to preserve the history of the country without writing.

Djuko instituted a new method of seating the parliament. Before his enthronement diviners prophesied that there would be a rebellion and advised him as to how he might avert it. "Have Mugema give you a child to seat the members of the council. The sinews of the person who will initiate you at Naŋkere will also help." The king informed the Mugema Semukoteka of all this. He asked that he give one of his sons for these duties. Mugema appointed his son Nagwala. The muscles of the person killed at Naŋkere were given him. They were dried and sewn into tight cowskin straps. These were to be used in whipping the people.

This position was very much respected, and parliament became much more dignified by the exercise of this power in preserving order. Several kings continued to recognize this as an hereditary function, and the office holders were all known as Nagwala. But during the reforms under Mutesa the office was abolished and the straps themselves buried.

EATING CUSTOMS.

In the old days cows were killed by striking the center of the head with an axe. But when the Arabs came in during the reign of Mukabya Mutesa and the king became a Mohammedan convert, this method was abolished, and that of slitting the neck introduced. Goats were always killed by slitting the throat and the blood was put in a bag of intestine lining and mixed with salted fat for cooking. This preparation was known as kafetce or luwampa. Usually it was not eaten until after the rest of the meat was finished. However, it was thought that if you cut a sheep with a knife and it saw you before it died, it would bring you bad luck and even death. Sheep were therefore killed with a heavy stick.

During the reign of Suna II the wealthy men acted in a very ceremonious fashion. At meal times, their wives washed their hands with sponges and then dried them with dry sponges. When the meal was served everyone waited until the chief had eaten. If a small child ate before its father did the mother was held responsible, and was fined a chicken.

A married man who was [a house owner, whether or not he was a chief, had a permanent seat,] known as Atenenya, meaning literally, "the one who does not repent", that is, if another man sat in the chief's chair he was obliged to offer an apology. [Not even a man's own son was permitted to sit on it,] (378) and was rebuked if discovered doing so, with the query, "Would you like to succeed your father while he is yet alive?" The job of keeping the seat exclusively for the chief was that of his wives, who were fined a goat for an offense such as placing a baby on it. It was even used as an excuse for divorce, or at least a separation of several months, after which the offending wife's relatives might bring her back with a payment. There is an old saying, "You are as troubled as a man in the seat of the chief."

CHAPTER XIII.

SACRIFICIAL METHODS,

Young [men who had misconducted themselves] at the capital, as by covering the streets with refuse or falling in love with a princess, [were liable to capture and slaughter. Sometimes the pretext was merely a superstitious one, the fortune teller having decreed the slaughter of an individual with a cataract or a white hand or some other such specific mark. In such a case the king might order his policemen out to arrest all those concerned and sometimes even some not concerned.] (331) This last was known as Kiwendo.

There were several people of different professions who were exempt from liability to this wholesale and capricious arrest.

Flutists, who always carried a bag for flutes as a mark.

Trumpeters, who always wore the trumpet tied about their necks.

Doorkeepers, who wore about their necks cane rings.

Potters, who carried small lumps of clay on their heads.

Cooks, who rubbed the bottoms of their barkcloths with mud.

King's servants, who had a special way of shaving their heads, and wore cane necklets, as did those of the prime minister, who were also exempt.

Butlers, who travelled with empty jars.

Priests in charge of the king's horns, who wore horns about their necks.

People of the Mamba clan, of the Bukerekere territory, were released, if they announced their clan, with the words, "You are free; go your way to your own death." If a member of this clan was arrested and put to death, Naŋkere might go and accuse the policeman before the king. He would immediately be executed.

Such was the complication in the execution of the king's duties, that they required permanent and expert officers who knew exactly what to do, and what not to do. Those assigned to these duties were henceforth free from any sort of punishment providing that they did their duties satisfactorily. Any other person who had none of the symbols noted above upon him might be brutally beaten or even murdered without cause. Travelers had to be careful to arouse no suspicion and in no way to provoke the policemen.

[All those thus arrested, and those previously confined, were sent to the sacrificial places known as Amatambiro and there killed, unless the king should send for one of them to be released.] (331) The number killed on any such occasion varied from one or a few up to several hundred, though the exact number is not known, as they were not counted..... This wholesale slaughter did not, however, decrease the population alarmingly, as did several religious wars and newly introduced diseases. This type of killing was done away with during the reign of Mukabya in 1876.........

[Sometimes the relatives of a man would try to rescue him by bringing two or three good looking girls to the king.] (332) If the case was not very dark, and the king was in good humor, he might

accept the fine and return the doomed man to his relatives. But if
the case was very serious and the king very angry, he would refuse
the request, nor would he in that case accept the girls offered him.
(R. says bribes to keepers were more common.)

The net of ropes in which a captured chief was bound was known
as eyakalira. [He was put in the stocks, but might retain considerable liberty by bribing the policeman,] (259) who simply made him
continue to wear the green head pad which was a sign of imprisonment, and guarded him a bit. He might have his wives with
him, and stay in a separate house. Some who were in prison for
as long as a year sometimes had children born to them.

[The period of confinement might end with release or slaughter.] (259) Having been somewhat at liberty all along, chiefs were led
to the slaughtering places without being bound. Their wives might
lead the way with a big jar of beer, from which they drank now and
again. [When the time for execution came the wife broke the jar](334)
and after the execution went home to detail the story to the other
wives and relatives.... (R. says chiefs were bound like others.) (334)

At the conclusion of these executions the king would refuse to be
interviewed except by the policemen and his young servants. When
the death journey began, the head of the procession would send
word to the king by a wise policeman as to who were the prisoners.
He would come before him and recite their names, laying down one
of the sticks he carried with each. When each of the prisoners had
been thus introduced, the king might name certain ones whom he
wished pardoned. The policeman threw away all the sticks but those
representing these and reported to the head captain. This was
repeated every day, those whom the king released being pardoned.
When the time for the slaughters came, the king was notified that
there could be no further communication. The next day all those
that remained were mercilessly killed.

Sometimes a sort of investigation was held first. The head captain
would ask each of them, "What was your case?" Hopeless as was
the situation, each proceeded to report. Then the captain ordered a
nine-handled [beer jar, and gave to each prisoner to drink out of
it.] (334) Then he announced to all of them, "It is not I who am
killing you, or who is giving you away to death, but Kibuka and
Mukasa are killing you." He also mentioned some other gods. The
reason the responsibility was thus shunned by the executioner and
the king was that they feared the ghosts of these men. Immediately
after this proclamation the prisoners were executed.

[There were several ways of putting these helpless victims to
death. Some were struck over the head with heavy axe-like sticks,

6

and had their arms and legs broken. Some had their heads cut off, and others, legs and arms amputated, were tied and left to become the prey of the buzzards. In some slaughter houses they were simply burned to death.](Methods varied with place and cause.)(334) The methods were very horrible. The prisoners were put into bundles of wood, piled into one heap and burned to death. [Some were carried to an island called Damba, had their legs chopped off, and were left on the rocks. The crocodiles, sensing a meal, would come and fetch them, already half dead, and devour them.] (336) Because of the tremendous number of slaughters and the scarcity of sacrificial places, some were taken to a small island called Mutukula in Siŋgo and there were drowned.] (337) The ladies and king's servants were differently treated. These were choked in the presence of the king or in the palace and the bodies were sent to their relatives.

There were two types of slaughtering places where the victims were burned to death. One group was for chiefs, princes, and princesses, and the other for the people. The first group consisted of the following places:

[Namugoŋgo	Kyadondo county] (337)
Busanyi	
or Djogero	Siŋgo county, at Buindja
[Beŋga	Buwekula county, near Mweŋge boundary.]

The second group consisted of the following places:

Kafunta	Kyagwe county, near Lake Kiira — (Nile)
Mpimerebera	Kyadondo county, at Busega, near Mayandja river

In all the other places the victims were killed by one of the other methods. The method of burning was considered rather an honorable one, so the royalty and aristocracy preferred that method. To be killed with a heavy blow on the head or stabbed with a dagger was considered rather degrading.

Because it meant death to a policeman to have one of his prisoners escape, they were watched very closely to avoid this. However, the policeman might evade the death penalty by bringing a fine of two of his best looking daughters or immediate relatives. If the king was pleased with them and received them it meant pardon.

THE HONORABLE CHIEFS EXEMPT FROM THE DEATH PENALTY.

Although the king had the power of killing each and every individual in the kingdom, here were those who by tradition were exempt from these penalties. These were:

Prime Minister
Kimbugwe, who had charge of the king's twin
Kago, Sabadju of Buganda
Mugema, the father of the king
Kasudju, the head nurse for the princes.

It was unlawful for a king to arrest, order, or do anything to these chiefs. Despite this tradition Tebutwereke arrested and murdered the Mugema Sentoŋgo. This act was a violation of the national tradition. When word of this went through the kingdom, the people rose in revolt and deserted the king and his kingdom. From their place of refuge they formed themselves into an army and returned to fight the king. He was overcome, killed, and his body was not honored with those of his fathers, but was thrown into the lake.

King Kyabagu also arrested and imprisoned his prime minister Kabinuli, but he soon released him.

King Semakokiro arrested his prime minister Kaduwamala because he had secretly borrowed a small string of beads known as Galuka from his wife Kikome. The king immediately ordered the policemen to put him in the stocks. During his confinement Kaduwamala died of the plague. The king was not willing to assume any responsibility in connection with his death. He ordered his body returned to his relatives, and everything which had been confiscated returned to his children. He stated, "I have not killed this man, he merely died of confinement in prison."

King Suna II murdered Kago Bulega for the furtherance of some mysterious plans.

King Mukabya arrested Kaira, the former Katikiro of Suna, and committed him to prison. He was compelled to accompany the doomed crowd and witness the horrible deaths. He himself was not killed because tradition forbade it. After a prolonged confinement he was given a small office, that of Seŋgoba, and released. He died while in this office. His arrest and imprisonment were caused by the machinations of some of his fellow chiefs who were jealous of his position. When the king grew to manhood, several chiefs approached him demanding Kaira's immediate dismissal, accusing him of violating the laws of the country by appointing several of his sons and relatives to office, on his own authority. The chiefs advised the king that he might be driven off the throne if all these sons and relatives should band together. Acting under this false and jealous advice, he arrested Kaira, deprived him of all his property, and imprisoned him. There was nothing to justify this action on the part of the king. When therefore he had fully grown into

6*

the wisdom of affairs, he repented of his action. As a recompense to the dead man he invited all his sons to visit him and honored them all by appointment to various offices.

Mukabya also arrested the Katikiro Mayandja, and ordered him imprisoned. He was handled very cruelly by the policemen, who kept him in the stocks day and night, so that he died. After his death the jailors came to the king with the false message that Mayandja had committed suicide. In denying any implication in the death, the king allowed the members of the Ŋkima clan to appoint his successor, and also showed his repentance by appointing Mayandja's sons to several offices in the country. The reason for his arrest was the same as that of Kaira's: accusation by his fellow chiefs because of his unusual position and intelligence. The allegation was that he did not eat entrails and that he was not actually a Muganda but a native of Budu country.

Mukabya also arrested and imprisoned Mugema Nakabale, and after his release deprived him of his position. Later, however, he reconsidered the case and reinstalled him. According to tradition no other clan might be given this office.

On the whole this killing reached terrible excesses. Sometimes the king put to death his own children, brothers, and sisters. Sometimes it was the other way round, several of the children conspiring together to kill their father. The chiefs killed their servants for next to nothing. The death penalty became so ordinary that it often put the chiefs in a dilemma.

THE HONORABLE LANDOWNERS EXEMPT FROM THE DEATH PENALTY.

There were two groups of chiefs who were thus honored. One group was allowed to see the king, but the other was traditionally barred from so doing.

In the first group was Kibale of the Mpewo clan at Kuŋgu, the kings aide. Although it was forbidden, King Suna II killed Kibale secretly, by torturing him in the stocks. The policemen claimed that he had committed suicide.

Others were:

Magunda	Fumbe clan, at Lwaŋga, who had charge of testing at the ordeals.
Sempala	Fumbe clan at Bulamba.
Kadjugudjwe	Butiko clan, at Bukerekere, priest of Nende.
Kaula	Lugave clan, the major drummer for Mudjaguzo.
Mbadzira	Nyonyi clan at Bulimo, the king's physican.

Masembe	Nsenene clan at Maya, the head shepherd, who looked after Namala, the cow that came with Kimera.
Namwama	Kobe clan at Buzimwa, the king's messenger for the bringing of the god Mukasa from Sese.
Kauŋga	Fumbe clan at Buwuŋgu, whose position it was to bring the god Wanema from Sese.
Mpiŋga	Lugave clan at Djokolera, the head of the king's police. During the reign of king Kimera, Mpiŋga killed the first person known to have been killed in the country. He was then removed from his position as shepherd and remained only a policeman.
Sebata	Ŋgeye clan at Mutundwe, who had been Kago, the king's aide. Later on he was made the second policeman.
Nabugwam	Mamba clan at Sambwe, who had once been Kaŋgawo.
Kinyoro	Ŋkima clan at Kisugu, who saved the jaw of King Djuko.
Mazige Sebuko	Mpindi clan at Muyendje, the second shepherd.
Semanobe	Mamba clan at Budo. He guarded Budo hill where the coronation ceremonies were held at first.
Lutaya	Ŋoŋge clan at Boŋgole, the guard of Kintu's tomb.
Kalibala	Nsenene clan at Nsisi, who had to buy a small grey antelope for the hunting trip of the new king, which was a commemoration of that of Kimera.
Mutasiŋgwa	Mamba clan at Kigwa.
Kiganda	Ŋoŋge clan at Biroŋgo, who had made a bond of blood brotherhood with Djundju before the Budu campaign.
Mudjambula } Lusundo }	Nvuma clan at Bugadja, who were priests of the god Wamala.
Natigo	Lugave clan at Magala. When Kimera returned from Bunyoro, Natigo was the first to talk to him, and then Kimera gave him the princely title.
Segirinya	Ŋgo clan at Lubandja was responsible for the sewing together of the king's twins and for bringing and changing the king's bed covers. He is still doing this.

The Honorable Land Owners who were not allowed to see the king:
(These had a considerable voice in the country.)

Buyoŋga Mugalula	Nsenene clan at Kisozi, the father of a daughter who was the mother of King Kimera.
Kadjubi Balitema	Nsenene clan at Kudjubi whose duty was to put a bead ring on the king's right hand and a white cowry just as he was crowned king. He was also Kasudju until Mutebi abolished this office.
Kalanzi	Nsenene clan at Lugo, the guard of the small barkcloth taken off the body of Kimera.
Mande	at Kabembe ⎫ ⎧ These three were the children
Djumba	at Bundjako ⎬ ⎨ of Mugema and were the play-
Kisambu	at Busambu ⎭ ⎩ mates of Kimera during his childhood in Bunyoro.
Mwaŋga	Ŋkima clan at Kyamuwoya
Nsamba	Ŋgabi clan· at Buwanda, the first baby to suck mother Wanyana, who afterwards gave birth to Prince Kimera, son of Kalemera.
Walusimbi	Fumbe clan at Baka, Sabadu of Tcwa Nabaka. When Tcwa disappeared he became temporary ruler. When he resigned, Sebwana became the ruler.
Naŋkere	Mamba clan at Kyandjove where kings became men.
Myamba Sebiso	Lugave clan at Ndugu was the chair carrier of the king, and up to this day his children are still counted upon for that job.
Kasudju	Ŋgeye clan at Busudju was considered the king's grandfather because his sister Nambi Nantutululu was the mother of Tcwa Nabaka.
Lwomwa	Ndiga clan, at Mbale, priest of Kibuka.
Mwandje	Ŋgo clan at Magoŋga, the chief landlord at Kintu's property up to today.
Kamyoka Mugalu	Mpindi clan at Nambeta.
Kamyoka Mugoba	Mpindi clan at Kiriŋgo.

The following Sese chiefs also did not see the king:

Kaganda	Ŋonge clan at Bukasa.
Semugala	Ŋkima clan at Bugala
Serumaga	Nvuma clan at Bwendero
Nyendje	Mamba clan at Kome
Namuyimba II	at Buyovu

| Gugu | Nvuma clan at Bubembe |
| Maso | Nvuma clan at Fuŋve. (This clan was also known as Bugeme). |

There were two reasons for the resolution of the chiefs of Buganda and Sese never to go to the royal court or to see the king. History shows that these chiefs were originally as much rulers as the king himself. Eventually several tyrannical kings reduced their power to that of mere chieftainship, which made them very indignant. Some of the chiefs had duties to perform at the coronation ceremonies, but after discharging these they returned home and were never again to see the king. Some kings continued their tyranny until it became unbearable. These chiefs were compelled to appoint their own sons to act as their prime ministers as representatives to carry their grievances before the king.

In order to distinguish these feudal chiefs, they wore brass rings around their legs and several hair crests on their heads. They were exempt from arrest for either civil or criminal offense.

During the reign of King Mutebi the feudal chiefs suffered violently. He murdered Kadjubi. Suna arrested Djumba, Mande, Myamba, and Namuyimba, and secretly murdered them. For fear of an open revolt, some of the chiefs were transferred to Busoga country, where they were put to death. The executioners returned with stories that the Busoga people had murdered them. In some cases the executioners were advised to choke, or kill them by other means, and bring the news to the king that they had committed suicide. Sometimes they were put to death through murder, during a war campaign. The news would come to the king that they had been killed accidentally while fighting, through not having been recognised. All these secret killings were due to fear. They could not be publicly executed, and the king feared that they might conspire, using the attitude of the people toward them as chiefs, and usurp the throne.

When a king pretended to be innocent of such a state murder, he ordered the relatives of the deceased to carry out all the regular funeral ceremonies with much pomp, and to have one of his sons succeed him. On the other hand, the king was afraid that if he did not honor the dead chief the ghost would haunt him.

When Mukabya Mutesa mounted the throne he abolished this custom altogether. He called these chiefs together and advised them to visit his court and guaranteed their positions. Those of the chiefs who were not satisfied continued wearing the brass rings on their legs and do so even up to the present time.

THE KING'S EATING AND FOOD DISTRIBUTION.

In olden times no one was allowed to eat food of which the king had eaten. Remains were all given to the dogs. This custom was followed also by some of the important county chiefs. Mawanda introduced a new procedure by inviting some young men of the Musu clan to dine with him. It was their duty to look after his latrines.

The usual distribution was of the following nature; the king invited the prime minister and certain of the other chiefs to dine with him, and to the rest of the chiefs who were in the public waiting hall he sent a large amount of mashed plantain food, and some beef, goat meat, and salt, each wrapped separately in barkcloth. He sent everything of which he ate, except that it was not considered proper for a man to send a chicken to a friend, as this was a disgrace to manhood. Kamanya however started the practice of sending his heroes chicken meat. Suna II, who was very fond of his chiefs, invited them to the porch of the dining hall and gave them all sorts of good things to eat, including chicken.

Mutesa did a great deal towards abolishing unnecessary old traditions. He too invited his chiefs to dine with him and distributed meat and other things to them. He required that the cooks be responsible for the serving of the meals. When he had distributed food to the chiefs he made sure that all the people who had come to be entertained were given sufficient food. After the meal beer was given them.

For the purpose of distribution the plantain food was divided into huge lumps. These filled five to ten baskets. There were also several pounds of meat. The people were seated according to position. The distributor saw to it that all the people were served. There was a special lump of food for special servants such as the Sababaki, which included the neck. The servants were not served until the king had retired. The cows used for the food belonged to the king and the shepherds brought them in turn.

When a chief made a contribution of beer to the king, it was poured into a large canoe-shaped container which was known as Tebiwulire. It was for the people employed in the palace. Each day after their work was done they came into the proper building and seated themselves and were all given beer.

CHAPTER XIV.

METHODS OF CONDUCTING WARFARE.

[All chiefs and their subordinates were invited to bring their armies for exhibition when the general was selected,] (348) in order that the proposed army might also be recruited from amongst them.

In the morning the king sounded his drum called Entamiv (drunkard) and all the chiefs assembled outside his house. While they all attended he came forward and announced the chief who had been appointed general. "Sekibobo" or any other chief, "you are the general. Go and fight such and such a country." [The appointed chief sprang to his feet and, brandishing his spear before the king, swore the oath of allegiance, "A man even a superman may attack me, but I shall utterly destroy him."] (349) Or he might say, "My name is Kimoga, I was born at Kuŋgu, I belong to the Mpindi clan. Any man whom I encounter I shall fight with to the death, as the shoes break the needle"..... This reference to the broken needle means that just as when a needle is broken it cannot be mended but must be discarded, so it is with a warrior when he is killed...........

When the newly appointed general returned home, he packed, and left for a five day vacation in the country. After this [he started for the war after selecting the wives who were to accompany him. When he left, his chief wives accompanied him, wearing grass about their necks.] (350) When the party came to a market place, [his chief wives,] Kadulubale, Kabedja, and Nasaza, [took their necklaces from their necks and put them about the necks of their husbands.......] (352)

[The grass from the spot where the warrior stood when bidding his wife goodbye was carefully saved] (352)......and whenever new grass for carpeting was brought in a little of this was added to it before it was spread. If the wife did not uproot this grass, she was allowed to cut no other grass and was considered a sorceress if she did so.... If the warrior returned home safely, she spread the grass she had saved on the seat were he was to sit while eating his first meal.

ARMY REVIEW.

[When the general and his army had crossed the boundary of the country, the whole army passed in review before him. This was his first chance to calculate the size of his army.] The review was conducted with regular military tactics. [The general was stationed at a particular place and each of the captains brought his division and swore the oath of allegiance,] (354) after which they passed the general laughing and shouting. This was the oath used: "When I meet the enemy, I shall not be afraid, but will fight with all my might." The soldiers painted their bodies with earth, and ashes and soot, and other disfiguring matter. Whenever they passed the general they repeated the oath, saying, "We will not look backward."

[The general adorned himself] (351) more conspicuously. Every morning when he went out for the march, he painted one side of his face with ashes, and the other with soot, and used chalk on his nose. This he did each day until they returned to Buganda. All the chiefs did this too, but the ordinary warriors might paint themselves as they chose.

The military uniform of the general, which was very varied from top to bottom, was rather a personal matter. [He wore a bunch of skins around his waist,] (351) the Kiteŋgu. These were colobus monkey skins woven together with long waving hair. Sometimes they were just skins of small animals. He wore a ring of beads around his neck and a [crown on his head] (351)......

This is how the army marched. At the left of the general the captains representing the following chiefs marched:

Pokino at the extreme end
Katambala next
Lubuga's assistant third
Kitunzi
Mukwenda last, next to the general

Kaima's division marched in front of the general, because the Pokino was the official Assistant Chief Guide. The warriors of the Katikiro also marched beside the general, and those of the general himself were in charge of the wives.

On the right hand side marched Kalabalaba, the Lieutenant General. This title means "The one who sees sharply" or a scout, and was conferred upon a favorite by the king himself. King Mukabya Mutesa abolished the title as part of his reforms, and appointed Omudjasi, the chief of police, permanently to this post.

Sekibobo; Kaŋgawo; Namasole's assistant; Kimbugwe's assistant; Kago, Sabadu of Buganda; Mugema, chief guard of the burial place; and Kasudju, chief nurse of the princes, marched behind the general. This formation was regularly observed until the homeward march.

[The custom of jumping over the chief's wife, Kadulubale, after the return of the army,] (351) was called the war's growth. Omission of this or any of the tabus in force during the period of the war proper, on the part of the general, was, it was believed, followed by lack of success on the part of the party in bringing back loot.

FOOD PLUNDERING.

[The army was fed by means of plunder]: (351) Each day before the march was resumed, the plunderers went ahead of the army, and looted as much food of all sorts as they could and brought it to camp. In dividing the food, portions were set aside for the general and the chief captains, and the rest was distributed among the army........

SCOUTING.

[The general would send a few men ahead to scout. If the army chanced to come in contact with the enemy, the general immediately divided his army and formed a defense. Where a thick battle raged, he put most of his warriors to fight.] (355) The division which consisted only of warriors without any carriers was called the raiders. At the spearing line the battle raged, and many of the warriors were killed. If the army won the defeated enemy was made to suffer greatly, their wives, servants, cattle, goats, sheep, ivory and anything else valuable they possessed being seized. All the men except mere children were put to death.

When the returning army was nearing camp, the division captain picked out of the spoil those things which he preferred. This was known as okukuba embwagula, and it was the first choice. It was in no way restricted. The captain might pick out a good looking woman, a cow, goats, servants, or anything else. According to their rank all officers in turn did this. After the distribution of all the loot, [the head captain led his army into camp and reported all events and developments during the campaign, and the loot his army had seized.] (359)

During the second distributing campaign, okukuba omuwambiro, the general picked out those things he most desired. This was done for him by the official messengers he sent, who were regular robbers, using their official power to take advantage of the warriors, who were unable to resist. Often a general would have five hundred women, two hundred servants, and a thousand or more cattle picked out for him. As in the first distribution, the captains and chiefs in order of their rank then made their selections. The total sum of all their acquisitions might number hundreds of women and servants and more than a thousand cattle. Goats however were left in possession of the men who looted them.

After the distribution of the loot, the general gave the order for the homeward march. Three or four days march away the general ordered his chiefs to search out a wide flat plain where everything might be checked. [A report was then sent the general of the findings.] (359) Thousands of women, a thousand or more slaves, and hundreds of cattle, might be reported. Then the general divided the spoils proportionally, more going to those who had looted more, by counties. This was known as okugereka, or to divide in proportion. He demanded a certain percentage of each reported item, 1000 out of every 3500 women, 4000 of every 10,000 slaves, 2000 of every 6000 cattle. These were the spoils of the king, but were left in the safe keeping of the chiefs. All the things which had been taken during the two other distributions they retained. The general might receive a total of 500 women, 200 slaves, and 1000 head of cattle. The captains might receive 600 women, 300 slaves, and 1200 head of cattle.

There were two exceptions to the general rule. The spoils of two captains' units were exempt from the authority of the general. These were the sections belonging to the queen mother and to Lubuga. If they looted more than 100 women, 50 slaves, and 250 head of cattle, these things were all returned to their respective chiefs, and they received only a compensation for their services.

THE WAR REPORT.

The cattle that were sent to substantiate the report sent the king were eaten by:

The queen
The throne attendants of the king
Kibale, the king's chamberlain
Nakatanza, the custodian of the king's horn Nantaba

Should there not be enough for all the above, the queen herself would be the beneficiary..........

In dividing the spoils, ivories received special treatment. They were not included in the lot sent with the special messenger but were secretly carried to the king by the general himself.

The grand total of all the war loot was known as "The Spoils". The share of the king in this has been as much as 3400 items, plus ten ivories, that of the general and the Katikiro's men 1300 items; the queen mother and Lubuga 800 items; the chiefs 2100 items; and 7100 for the warriors, making a total of 14,700. The king's cattle men received their share and took them over to the cattle fold. Any one whose fold was almost exhausted would share in this bounty.....

This custom of robbing the surrounding nations brought wealth to the Baganda, but it also meant loss of their ability to trade. These expeditions had to be made quite regularly about every six months, and sometimes resulted in considerable loss of life and no particular gain.......

There was also a private sort of warfare which might be undertaken by chiefs living near the border, on their own accounts......

Should the test of the wife's fidelity (by drinking a special decoction) (362) prove positive and the returned warrior be made ill by it, the neighbors would advise the wife to give him special medicines. His cure contradicted the test. [If he persisted in his charges the wife was expected to name the partner of her adultery. If the man was found and found guilty he was made to suffer for it, especially if a wife of the king were involved.] (362) If the accusing husband's sickness continued for a long time it was thought to have been caused naturally, and the wife was declared innocent.......

Upon the return of the warriors, their wives went to meet them with cups of water. If a peasant woman was informed of the death of her husband, she smashed the cup to the ground, and went home crying with her hands turned upwards. It became unlawful for anyone to smash a cup, jar, or other clay pot in the yard while the owner of the house was still alive. The act was always done in connection with the death ceremonies.

If a man ran away from the war in fear and was caught, the general immediately ordered him burnt, as an example to the other people, since this was considered a very cruel way to die..... [There was a more elaborate investigation in the case of chiefs.] (361).....

[Should such a shirker not be punished by death, he was dressed like a woman.] Also a bit of the decayed pith of a plantain stem was bound behind him in imitation of a woman giving birth. [He was taken about that the people might see what treatment a coward might expect. Finally he was put in charge of one of the courageous officers, taken home and put to woman's work.] (362) He was obliged to prepare meals, fetch water, and so forth. The worst part was that he was required to prepare a meal of chicken and carry it on his head and deliver it to some of the army officers, carrying it several miles..... [A chief was expelled from his office, which was entrusted to the braver men. He was made to serve as their servant.]......

Part of [the ceremony by which a father honored a son returning as a hero from war] (363) was a benediction recited while he embraced him. "May the gods and the ghosts of your forefathers bless you and keep you in this world and the world to come." The meal which followed was shared by all the family, the son being fed by his father through it all.......

CHAPTER XV.

COLLECTING THE KING'S TAXES.

Buganda history shows that in the middle ages the tax was collected in the form of grain and beads. These were displaced when the use of cowry shells as money was discovered. There are several theories as to how the people secured the things which were formerly used.

The following is a list of the various sorts of taxes imposed:

Kikuŋgo — This was a [live stock tax.] (244) Every one had to pay one of every twenty cattle, and one of every twenty goats.

[Barkcloth tax] — Every one who could not pay this had to pay 250 cowrie shells.

Bakitatabala or non-fighters tax. All males who did not participate in the wars had to pay a tax of 250 cowrie shells, or a barckloth and five cowrie shells.

Those who imported salt from the Bunyoro country had to pay a tax on it.

Those people who lived in the region where there was an annual ant-hill season, were taxed a full vessel of ant-hill per family. From this has been coined the proverb, "This is the ant-hill tax, you feed upon it while taxing." This meant that no one could count the dead ants, and there was no one to find out about it.

The Sese islanders were taxed in fish.

Each family was taxed a full vessel of eggs and another of semsem. Some times the chiefs themselves went in person to collect this tax.

Those states near the Bunyoro country paid their taxes in hoes which were well and cheaply made by the Banyoro.

Folk who owned ten to twenty-five acres were expected to pay a tax of a worn-out hoe.

Several chiefs shared the duty of providing the king with women singers at all times.

Baskets were brought in quantities to the king, as were hoe-shafts.

[Clay potters,] known as Abadjona, [were brought to make the royal vessels, pots, etc.] They were put in charge of Banda. [The band of clay potters grew very numerous, as their children too were retained in the trade.] (399) There are very few of them at present.

There was one very peculiar tax. When a chief's family suffered death or defeat, or any misfortune, all his servants were taken from him and distributed by the king among the other chiefs. Some of these who were very able might have the luck to be themselves appointed chiefs.

A tax was imposed upon the aged men. They were brought to the royal palace to serve as guards for the king's wives. They were called Abatete.

The subordinates of the following chiefs were exempt from taxation:

The queen
The queen mother
The prime minister
Kimbugwe, the twin keeper
Kibale, the king's chamberlain.

They collected the taxes themselves and paid a certain amount to the king. Where the above officials had their estates the people in charge of the estates shared with their masters, their share being known as Obukumandagala.

Taxation in Buganda affected only the mass of the people. [The chiefs and their immediate subordinates were exempt.] (244) The only obligation on their part was what was called Bugenyi. This was given to the tax collector by the chiefs. A Saza chief gave two cows and the lesser chiefs gave one each. Other persons exempt from taxation were the assistant chiefs, the close relatives of the king, bachelors, and all families that had just moved to newly settled land, whose first crops had not yet been reaped.

[When the collected tax was being redistributed] (245) the proportions would be somewhat as follows. Of 430 bundles, [after the collecting chiefs had subtracted their shares]:

[The Saza chief who sent them   150
The prime minister]   60
Kimbugwe   7
Kibale   5

(These latter two have this privilege only since the time of Mukabya Mutesa.)

The messenger then carried the rest of the bundles to the king. He gave 84 to the messenger, 7 each to Sabakaki, the head of the servants, and Mulamba, the head doorkeeper. The remaining bundles were for the king himself.........

The following states owed tribute to Buganda:
Busoga, and Kiziba

The Banyoro and Banyaŋkole paid no actual tax, but gifts were made by them in great number........

Until the reign of King Suna II all the king's wealth was in charge
of the Katikiro. During his reign Kaira, who was Katikiro, became a
drunkard, and gave away some of the king's property. He was
compelled to transfer his treasury into the palace, where it still
remains. The Katikiro retained his position as treasurer, and as
such entertained the king's visitors and disbursed such goods as
gifts as the king might order.

Often the king had a favorite, whom he ordered to be given ten of
everything, and anything more that he wanted, so that he might
become rich. When he left the palace, people would know of the
friendship of the king for him and would do him honor.

[There were several special ways of addressing the king which the
chiefs used.] These were, "You gave me your majesty," or "Only
yourself, husband," or, "I did see you," or, "The burning plains".
A chief would address his peers with the name of the king. The idea
was that they owed their power and its protection to the king and
so he ought to be remembered at all times.

Women and servants were not allowed to answer as the chiefs
did. They simply answered, "Yes, sir," even as they do today. It was
an act of disloyalty to say anything further as this pretended to
greater recognition than was accorded them.

When a person received anything from the king, he had to
express his gratitude, saying, "I am very thankful, sir," or, "I am
very appreciative, your majesty, that I have received of your power,
that which broke the axe and re-mended it." In thus offering thanks
one had to stretch oneself on the ground, rubbing your chin on the
ground, or kneel with your hands gracefully clasped behind your
back. Then you must jump to your feet and shout humourously,
"You have given me your majesty." Should a friend meet you and
call your name, you must say, "I have met his majesty."

FINES.

[Any chief who failed to perform his duties was liable to a heavy
fine,] (259) imposed upon him by a royal messenger sent directly to
his home to announce it. These fine collectors were supposed not
to sit down or to eat anything until their business had been trans-
acted. The amount of the fine was in accordance with the wealth of
the chief. The messengers were so highly honored that as a rule
whatever they said was accepted without complaint. It was not
until the fine had been paid that the messenger explained the reason
or it.

The messenger returned to the king and presented to him the

fine, saying, "I have fined such and such a chief for failure to perform such and such a duty." The fines were divided among the king, the Katikiro, the messenger, and the Saza chief, unless the last named was himself the one fined.

When the fine was a very heavy one for the chief, he would send for his friends to assist him. Sometimes the fine consisted of 100 women, 100 cattle, 100 bundles of barkcloth, to be paid within fifteen days.....

CHAPTER XVI.

THE KING'S CHAIRS.

Formerly the king used to sit on a cow skin known as Ebiwu. This word is of foreign origin, borrowed from the Luima language, in which a skin is called Luwu. The mother of Kimera, the first king to use such a seat, was Wanyana, a Muima.

[Later a chair was made, known as Namulondo. It was made when King Mulondo succeeded his father.] (197, 408) His prime minister, Sekagya, conferred with Gundju the king's uncle to make a chair wherein the king might sit for all the people to see him.... Namulondo is really the throne and is highly respected..... The following chiefs were in charge of the throne:

> Mwotasubi   of the Ŋkima clan
> Kiwukyeru   of the Fumbe clan
> Mutagwanya of the Butiko clan
> Lukwanzi   of the Mpindi clan

[The throne house was on the right hand side of the palace gateway.] (Appendix) All persons but the relatives of the guards were excluded from the throne house.

King Djuko was credited with having been the first to construct raised seats. These were rectangular constructions, made of mud, five feet long by four broad, and three feet tall. [Dry grass was spread on this, and a leopard skin and barkcloths.] (258) The king could then be immediately recognised by anyone coming to the court. This type of throne was called Kituti. Little ones were constructed at every public place where the king appeared. The people of the Lugave clan were responsible for building and for guarding them. These seats were used until the introduction of chairs under Mutesa. They did not really disappear until the reign of Mwanga II. Captain Speke, the first white man to visit the country, gave a chair as a gift to Mutesa........

7

When the king desired to move his seat temporarily, or when he was journeying and happened to be watching a game, he sat on the laps of his chiefs or servants. When Mutesa became king he ordered his blacksmiths to make several steel chairs, and the carpenter to make several wooden ones. These he placed in the council house for the use of his chiefs. There were four hundred of these, and half of them were ranged on each side of the house. The king sat in the center of the house, the prime minister next to him, then Kimbugwe, and after him the Saza chiefs.

It was King Semakokiro who added [lion and hyena skins to the throne. They are still used today.] (197) The throne was not used very often but was used for such special occasions as the customary feasts, declarations of war, or the return of the army from war. [The king sat in state to announce his royal decrees, either in the center of the gateway] (360) or at the house of the queen.

[The king's sandals were sewn with thongs of leopard skin. The sandal for the prominent princesses and the queen mother were also made that way.] (409) Some old-fashioned members of the royal family still wear these today. It was an act of disloyalty for the princes or the chiefs to wear such sandals.

The place where the king resided even temporarily was called the palace, Busiro. It was said that when Tembo became king he founded his palace on Busiro hill, meeting his chiefs and the public there. It became a common expression for those who had seen the king to say, "We have seen the king at Busiro hill." Later the name came to be applied to all places where the king was, [and to the burial places for the kings.] (252)

All the edible things belonging to the king were known as Amakula. When the king was at the royal meals, the expression was used, "There is Amakula at the royal court," or else, "The baskets are still at the royal court." The former was used only of royalty and only the latter could be used of ordinary chiefs. When Suna II became king, he was very fond of his prime minister, Kaira, and gave him the name, "You are all in all the outside king." Because of this all the foodstuffs he used took the name applied to the royal things.

CHAPTER XVII.

MARRIAGE.

When Suna II became king he ordered that anyone that wronged a young girl be put to death. This caused the people to be very careful. But during the reign of Mukabya the coming of the Arabs caused the breakdown of these customs. They also introduced sodomy.

COURTSHIP.

[On the whole this account agrees with that of Roscoe except that
it is the aunt who plays the role of go-between that he assigns to the
brother.] (87—89)........

[The cowry shells paid by the groom during the ceremony of
marriage were returned to him to make it apparent to him that the
transaction which had taken place was in no sense a purchase.] If
the father and the other relatives of the girl were inconsequential
people they might actually want to exchange her for money. If
they kept the shells the husband understood that there was another
payment to be made and that then the woman would be his property.

If a chief received word that there was a good-looking girl among
his people he might notify her parents that he wanted to marry her.
The complicated courtship was omitted. If the parents were satisfied they sent their daughter to the chief, who sent them as a
deposit five jars of beer, two cows, two goats (known as good-
morning), two bundles of barkcloth, two baskets of salt, and five
thousand cowry shells. These things were consumed by the family,
because it was understood that the wife of a chief was never divorced, and that therefore they would never have to answer for them.

Ten days before the wedding (Roscoe says several weeks) (89)
the [girl was washed and coached by her mother in her social
relationships and in household routine. There were several superstitions in connection with this period of the "marriage preparation".] (89) If it rained or a jackal called it was considered a bad
omen and the wedding was called off, or one of the parties to it
would soon die. These were called omens of "tearful mourning".

[A place was set at which the parties were to meet for the
marriage ceremony.] (86) The chief did not participate himself but
sent a representative. The bride's party hid her and demanded
100 cowry shells. The bride was then put in a conspicuous place
and her sister, taking her by the right hand, offered her to the
representative, saying, "Here is your woman, take her."....
(Roscoe says that the ceremony is the same for the chiefs as for the
commoners.) (86)........

The bride's goat was a regular part of the ceremony. The liver
was roasted and brought to her. The bride and groom both ate of
it as a symbol that he recognised her as his real wife. Those women
who did not share the liver with their husbands were merely concubines. After this the chief had intercourse with his wife. [If she
was found virgin, he ordered the blood of the bridal goat sprinkled
on a barkcloth.......] (91)

7*

[Shortly after the marriage the wife working in the garden was given a present of cowries] as a symbol of her husband's approval. (Roscoe says this is a sign of the mother-in-law's acceptance.).....

[After three months the bride returned home] with the bridal dress and a package of salt and one of [butter. She handed the butter to her father] or if he was dead, to his successor. If they were not at home, she might not bother with the butter. Later she went to the home of her sister or some other immediate relative and got [some chickens and plantain food, which she prepared as a token of love for her husband....] (91) A chief's daughter brought a cow, or two goats, instead. This still prevails, even after Christian marriage.

When a [man paid a fine for the return of a wife who had left him] (92) and she continued to remain at the home of her parents he might accuse her relatives before the county chief of refusing to release his wife. He might even carry the case to the court of the Katikiro. If the decision was in his favor, a representative was sent to force the wife to return to her husband. (Roscoe says divorce could be effected by return of the dowry.) (92, 97).

If a divorced woman remarried and got into trouble again a divorce was easily arranged. It was during Suna's reign that the custom of killing an adulteress was introduced. There was an institution known as the love test. The husband's brothers-in-law demanded ten goats, which they immediately returned, as the object was merely to find out whether he was in love with their sister. If the man did not have the amount demanded he might borrow it from his neighbors. The men made him produce three women as "children". He presented these to the brothers-in-law, who said to the women, "Here is your child! If he misconducts himself in any fashion, you will be responsible." When they accepted the responsibility the man served beer to the brothers-in-law, and they all made merry. It was assumed that the man would now meet all his domestic obligations.

[After marriage a man was not allowed to see the mother or any other of the female relatives of his wife. They were all called Bakodomi, Untouchable.] (129) A woman was not allowed to touch her father-in-law or her brothers-in-law. When visiting them she walked around the yard instead of going through it. She was not allowed to hand anything to them. However, she was allowed to meet her mother-in-law, sitting at a distance of about six feet. If a man touched his daughter-in-law, even by chance, a subsequent illness would be ascribed to the breaking of the taboo.

[A man was also forbidden to touch the child of an aunt.] (129)

This was known as Kizibwe. If a cousin happened to be in the house when a man had intercourse with his wife, this violation might cause illness. Such an act would demand the sacrifice of a white goat, a chicken, and two white grains. These were taken to the outskirts of the plantation and there cooked and eaten. The person who was in the house at the time of the violation bound the two grains on the hands of the sick person and said, "If it was touching me that caused all this trouble, I have forgiven you and hope you will get well." If the person recovered he had to avoid the other again. If he did not it was understood that something else had caused the trouble..........

[It was unlawful to marry into one's mother's clan,] (128) especially into her immediate family. [It was unlawful to marry anyone in one's father's clan,] (128) who ranked as a sibling. Any one who committed incest was taken to Luwube in Bulemezi and there killed at the slaughtering place Kubamitwe. (Roscoe says it was here that the king killed adulterous wives) (337) or at Balita at Busubika in Bulemezi. (Roscoe says those who committed incest were killed at Ekule on Busiro.)

[When a man had a child by a girl who was not married, he was fined a goat,] (79) upon which the girl, her parents, and the man feasted. The women served each other as did the men. After the meal the father jumped over his wife and the boy over the girl. It was believed that otherwise the father would die.

CHAPTER XVIII.

WOMEN'S TABOOS.

[There were several varieties of vegetables and fruits which a pregnant woman might not eat...] (48) When these taboos were violated and the child died the family of the husband became very angry and punished the wife by beating her, so that she would not make the same mistake again.

[The menstrual period was known as peace. The woman in this condition was not allowed to touch anything and to go where she liked.] (95) Since this was a time during which she was supposed to do nothing the word was applied to any loafing. Non-observance of these taboos affected the ability of the woman to bear children. (Roscoe says it is the growth of her garden that is affected.)......

A woman who died at childbirth through the neglect of the customary precautions was supposed to have been inadequately cared for by her husband. Her family fined him two women, two cows, and some other things......

If a mother or a father wronged another person during the time between the birth of their child and its naming, the child would die. In order to help it an emetic was administered. When it recovered the spouses accused each other of misconduct. If the medicine failed to cure, it showed that the sickness was due to some other cause and the parents were innocent. This procedure was known as okukansira. Because of this belief the parents were very [careful to have no intercourse with anyone else until after the naming ceremony.] (55)

If this period coincided with the grasshopper season a woman whose husband was away was not allowed to go out to gather them lest the child die. If he were at home he had to be reported to after the gathering. She had to say to him, "Here are some of the grasshoppers." Then she prepared a good grasshopper meal, after which her husband jumped over her, or they had intercourse. If a woman forgot to tell her husband the child would die.

It was customary for a pregnant woman to remain with her husband for six or seven months. This applied only to the common people, since the chiefs never lived with any particular wife but visited all of them in turn. The chief had his official headquarters at the home of the head wife, Kadulubale. From here he visited his other wives, staying perhaps ten days with each or as much as a month with a wife who was a particular favorite. During the reign of Mutesa this was abolished and the chief was visited in turn by his wives at his own dwelling house.... If a woman remained here for a particularly long time the others merely said, "So and so is the favorite of the chief, she remains at his house a long time." When one of the wives had been pregnant for about three months she was taken to a place where she was in charge of a special servant.

[When the time approached the woman was rubbed with butter mixed with medicine,] (54) from the back, around the ribs, and down to the stomach. This was to balance the child and strenghten its passage. Ten days or less before the birth she was made to sit in a special medicine with her legs stretched out before her. For this reason the medicine was called, "It breaks the bones"..........

[A reed was ordinarily used for cutting the cord.] (52) Often, though, the umbilical cord of a boy was cut on a spear shaft, that of a girl on her mother's hoe. The second cutting took place after three days for the boy, four for the girls. (Roscoe says it was after nine days.) (55)

[A baby that was born feet first was known as Kidjananeŋge, or extraordinary creature.] If it died (Roscoe says that it was strangled) [it was buried by the wayside.] A baby born with a harelip was called Nakim, or the lone one.

There were several diseases peculiar to babies. There was a throat disease which was supposed to infect the chest all the way to the navel, in which all the blood vessels and the stomach swelled up, so that the baby was not able to take nourishment. Then the father took it in his right hand and went, all naked, to burn a bush. The ashes he rubbed about the mouth of the baby. For a girl the uncle did all this. For this disease the mother spat a medicine, which she had chewed, all over the baby's stomach..........

When during a journey a man and his wives came to their destination the wives brought all the baby's rugs and piled them under those of the husband. He jumped over them all, and over the chief wife. If he had intercourse with other women before the ceremony, the child might die. If the one with the baby went with the man he was obliged to fulfill the custom with her before knowing the other, even if he did not love her........

[The salt for the naming ceremony] (62) was prepared by putting some leaves in a strainer, and on these the [ashes of burned egugu grass]. Water was strained through this and then put in a vessel to be kept for [use as salt] (62). This process was known as oku-gunekera. For this feast in addition to the vegetables a male and a female goat were prepared, and if the child was a chief's a cow, or even several of them, might be killed.......

[The umbilical cords were fastened to the children for this ceremony,] the boy's around the right, the girl's around the left hand. The children were seated on their mothers' laps..... The father and his elder brother had their meal inside, and food was sent out to the mothers. A lump of plantain food was set down on the mat, and only after this was eaten was the [legitimacy test performed] (62). (Roscoe says that a feast, which the mothers do not attend, follows this.) (63)........

[Should the result of this test indicate that the woman had been guilty of adultery, she would be punished. A common man would beat his wife.] (64) A chief however would wait for the result of the test to be confirmed by the sickness and death of the illegitimate child.......

[When the ceremony of naming was concluded the children were washed] and the water splashed over their mothers. Then each woman put two lumps of flour and a fish in leaves, and ate of it. They also gave some to the children, with much shouting and rejoicing. After this the...... [umbilical cord was buried.] (62) The following song was sung:

"A little rotten log is always responsible for banking the fire." This means that when a child begins to grow strong he is as the fire,

while the mother, who had exercised care during pregnancy, is
as the log.

There was some local variation in the naming ceremonies. The
county Kyagwe and the Mpindi clan had the most distinctive ones.
(Roscoe says the method of disposal varies with the clan.) The
ceremonies for the naming of twins were quite different......

[Scarification was introduced first in Kyagwe county and then
spread,] (87) but the princesses and members of the Nsenene clan
never adopted it. The latter considered themselves nobles by virtue
of descent from Kimera. The clan ancestor Buyoŋga was a Muima.

Women also decorated themselves by boring a hole in the lower
lip through which the saliva might flow when they were smoking.
This style, also introduced through Kyagwe, did not spread the way
scarification did.

Some old women had large jars for the storage of smoked meat.
They were called kitafuka and no one was allowed to touch them.
There was a coffee-grain basket called endabi which was also taboo.
Transgression of this rule meant sudden death to a child born to the
offender. When a child suddenly died the father consulted a diviner
as to the cause. Should he say that the mother had touched a coffee
basket which was not her property the husband would come home
and question her. He would give her a white goat and a white cowry
shell to give to the offended owner of the basket. This person would
then touch the woman, saying, "Never again touch a coffee basket
which does not belong to you." — "I shall never do it again," the
wife would reply.

There were several traditional observances required of women
which were indicative of their respect toward men. For instance, if
a boy, even a very young one, came in while people were eating,
what food was given him was handed him on a leaf, or set where he
could reach it himself after washing his hands. A woman never
walked over her husband's weapons, particularly the spear, for
such an action would result in its unsuccessful use by the husband.
If a man went to battle and was killed as the result of his wife's
ill-advised action, she was considered a witch.

When the warriors were leaving for war, their friends bade them
goodbye, saying, "Mubataŋge Bukazi" — "Kill them as women"...

It was unlawful for a woman to announce the death of a sheep.
She was responsible for the pasturing and stabling of the live stock.
(Roscoe says that only the men could tend the cattle but the taboos
surrounding goats were not so rigorous.) (417.) Should she find
that a sheep had died she had to say to her husband, "There is one
of your sheep I am not able to let in. Come and help me."

[Women were forbidden to taste sheep,] (473) chicken, lung fish, hog, and some fish. Eggs and small fish might be eaten by noble women. Any woman who broke this taboo was laughed at by her fellows. Even today there are some who continue to obey these restrictions.

CHAPTER XIX.

TWINS.

. . . .

The children who were appointed Saloŋgo and Lubuga for the twins might never again see the father of the twins, but must always run away from him. . . . . .

[The man whose function it was to shut the door] had a special shave after [the ritual stealing of the bananas]. A strip was shaved from his forehead straight over his head to his back, and then a cross strip was shaved. Small bells were tied on his legs and on those of some of his friends. They were then allowed to take anything they liked from any of the gardens.

[Saloŋgo, or the husband, as he was called,] might not strike anybody, nor kill a goat. He [was not allowed to see blood. His meals were all of the unmashed plantain food](66) until the formal feast upon a goat, which was known as Mugereŋgedjo. [During the following month a drum was sounded every day.] (65) Then his brothers and other relatives were requested to make dancing costumes of palm leaves, and their wives to make some of ordinary leaves. The little husband was given a crown to wear. The next morning the father went out to the house of all his friends and cast at each a token of his friendship.

[After the lapse of a month, and at the appearance of the moon, he killed a goat, and the feast mentioned above was held.] (68) Everybody had to be careful to do no wrong. Anyone found having intercourse with a woman could have no share in the feast. . . . . . .

If the twins died immediately after birth they were not buried at once. Their corpses were tightly wrapped in a grass called Bombo. The mother then put them behind the cooking pots for embalming by means of the heat of the fire, which was not an altogether satisfactory method. The mother and all her children were required to remain behind the cooking pots until the head chief came to take the corpse for burial. The next day he would come early in the morning and knock at the door, saying, "Are you all in ?" — "Yes," the reply would come back, "We are in." Then the visitor would tell them that the day had already dawned, and open the door. The

Salongo or husband then came out, and they greeted each other saying, "Gauga", which greeting concluded the ceremonies.

If on the other hand the twins remained alive, it was the after-birth that was put behind the cooking pots. If they died after the lapse of a month only the ordinary burial ceremonies were performed.

After the chief had returned to his home the husband brought out his three big drums, Eŋkalabirizi, Kaŋgudjuŋgudju, and Kakalabu, which were all dance drums, and sounded these and danced. He also went to the temple of the priest who had prophesied the birth of twins and there played his drums and sang...........

During the feasting time following the birth, food was prepared in special fashion. Mostly goat and chicken meat were used. The insides of the goat were removed and the animal roasted whole, with the feet and the skin still attached. Chicken was cooked in like manner, except that the feathers were removed.........

[When the children had been given their names, the parents took their umbilical cords and the tongue of a white chicken] (70) and mixed these with a grass known as bombo, a grain, and some of the excrement of a child. [These were wrapped in barkcloth and known as the twin.] (70)

[When all these customs had been observed, Salongo went to his father to break a second Lukanda.] (72) This was done wherever his father happened to be at the time. The father congratulated his son and gave him gifts. The son might refuse to accept these if he did not think them sufficient. He might give two cows and two women, but a poor man might be able to give only one cow. After giving the gifts to his son the father went into the house and shut the door. On it he hung withered plantain leaves. [The next evening Salongo brought a goat and left it in the house. His father then killed it for a feast.] (71) The next morning the father came out with a liquid chalk known as doŋgo and sprayed it all over his son and all those who were with him. During this ceremony all sang. Some of the songs were the following:

"The owner of the house waits in woe. We are bringing Salongo. Stand in woe here, we are bringing the twins for you."

Another

"Let the drum sound, Sewaswa, the father of twins.
They are sounding, they are sounding.
Sewaswa's drums are sounding,
Sewaswa's drums are sounding among his twins."

A third

"Here is his homeland, here where the twins are.
Here is his homeland, here where the twins came from."

There were also many other songs, but some of them are so
absurd that it was impossible to include them in the book. There
were also cheers, "Usi, Usi, Saloŋgo. Usi and Naloŋgo, Usi."
[When the dancing was over they all entered the house for the
feast. The father handed his daughter-in-law a lump of plantain
food] (71) and thanked her for being the mother of two children. . . .
In response the woman handed over to her mother-in-law the second
lump of plantain food, thanking her for her appreciation. . . . . Then
the father blessed his son and his wife and their children, and told
them to return home. . . . . After the feast the second Lukanda was
over, and they all returned to their homes.
[The third breaking of Lukanda was before the king. This was
done by the chiefs. . . . A chief took with him a small jar of beer, and
was preceded by the beating of his drum. He met the king at the
palace gateway. He handed him the jar of beer,] (72) and the king
in return said, "Today I have invited you to bring your children,
and I have decreed that from now on you shall be termed Saloŋgo
in token of having had twins." Saloŋgo replied, "I thank you, my
lord, for inviting me and giving me this name." This custom was
followed because from the time twins were born to him a chief was
no longer able to see or eat with the king. The day that this ceremony was performed meant his restoration to his former position
and privilege. When a chief came to have this ceremony performed
he always brought several gifts for the king. The king would appoint
his chief, Mugema or Kago, to receive them for him. These two
chiefs were the ones who acted as deputies in any ceremony when
the king did not attend in person. Mugema was Sabadu, or chief
of all the king's burial places. Kago was Sabadu for the living
king. . . . .
The other "twin", which was bound, was part of the after-birth.
This was sometimes worn. It was decorated with beads. Even [today
there may be found at Busiro the "twins" of kings, chiefs, and other
people.] Every child of the king had such a twin made. These twins
were very dear to the people. When one of them was destroyed
by the burning of a house they would make another from the first
thing which fell into a barkcloth spread for the purpose. This was
immediately bound and decorated and used as a twin. (Roscoe has
this done as part of the ceremony when one of a pair of real twins
dies, in order to make a mate for the other.) (124)

The mass of custom and belief surrounding the birth and life of twins made the attitude of parents to whom they were born rather a mixed one. Some chose to kill them off. In that case none dared to say they had been killed or even that they had died, but said instead that they had gone to heaven. (A circumlocution which according to Roscoe is used at the death of a twin from any cause.) (124)

CHAPTER XX.

FOOD TABOOS.

During the harvest season, the women planted millet. It was harvested, ground, and prepared for consumption when ripe. Before the first meal of the season might be made of it, the husband had to kill a goat. Then it was eaten, and the remainder of the millet dried. After this the man jumped over his wife. (Roscoe has procedures of the same sort in connection with the bean harvest.) (428).

When semsem was ready for the harvesting, it was gathered at a "bee". The husband prepared a large rack for storing it. When the woman and her friends had gathered the semsem, the man had to pay a fine if the rack was too small. This consisted of one goat. When there was not enough of the grain to fill the rack, the woman paid her husband a chicken. If the husband wished to acknowledge the diligence of his wife, he paid her the goat even if the results did not demand it.

When the semsem was dry the woman collected her friends once more to winnow it. She put two worn barkcloths under the rack, and the husband, with a stick to which a special grass was tied, beat down one [bunch of the semsem. This was thrown away at a crossroads, that the passersby might be reminded to bless the next crop.] (433) Then the husband began to beat at the grain, and the others went on with the winnowing......

When a woman went out to cut down a bunch of plantains she scraped the bloom or powder on the young stems of the cluster and rubbed this at the spot where she had cut the tree. This was supposed to insure the continuous growth of the plantain tree.

CHAPTER XXI.

DEATH CUSTOMS.

When the king died his body lay in state for about four weeks and all his relatives came to mourn. (Roscoe says that the body was kept only for a day or two.) When a king died the attendants seized the limbs and straightened the corpse. The body was washed and placed upon new barkcloth on the floor. It was laid face upward and the arms and legs were straightened. Then the body was squeezed and barkcloth applied. After this the middle wall of the house was torn down, as were the other walls. It was covered with raw plantain leaves, and the body was placed in the centre.

After this all the meals were prepared in the yard. Dry fences were used for the purpose of cooking and the mourners slept not on beds but on the floor.

[In a few days the entrails were removed and bathed in strong beer. Then they were replaced and the body was tightly tied.] (105) There were three guards placed on each side of the body, [whose duty it was to squeeze the body now and then, using sponges and very strong beer.] (105) Each part was tightly wrapped to prevent the setting in of decomposition. [This was continued until the body was all dried, when myrrh was applied.] (105) The head was tied to the body to prevent its dropping off.

[The best loved wives of the deceased were given the beer which had been used in the washing to drink.](105) They were told, "Here is your husband. Consume him in death as you did when he was alive." Then they all went into the house and lamented. The tortures to which the wives of chiefs were subjected were so great that the women hoped rather for the death of their parents than of their husbands. (Roscoe does not make any distinction between the funerals of ordinary people and of chiefs.)

[A princess who died was not buried until one of her male relatives died and was buried first.] (116) From this has come the Baganda proverb, "A woman never preceded a man to the grave."

A large payment had to be given the men who did the embalming. Ninety women, ninety servants, and ninety cows was the usual sum for the king, less for the princes, and nine of each for a chief.

There was a conference after the death at which all the relatives took part. This was to determine the cause of the death of their kinsman, since most people believed there could be no such thing as natural death. The deceased was believed to have been bewitched or in some way magically harmed, as by the placing of medicine on the road where he used to walk; or to have been haunted by the malevolent ghost of a vengeful injured relative; or to have suffered for the violation of the oath of blood brotherhood, or some unrequited quarrel, theft, or other misdeed on his part. It was not till after the cause of death had been settled that the eldest brother acting as spokesman set the place for the burial.......

[Before the burial and over the body there was a second conference, to pick the heir.] (119) A brother or some other near relative of the same generation was selected, rather than a son. Apparently the latter was considered to be the less close of the relationships, or the relatives feared prejudiced attitudes or innovations on the part of the son... This was abolished during Mutesa's reign, and the king approved the succession of the son instead.....

[The eldest son, or a grandson, spat pumpkin seeds over the body and the grave, and then at the one of the wives of his father] (117) whom he liked best. This woman was to become his wife. This ceremony was a sort of advertisement of the fact that the man had progeny. It was somewhat of a disgrace for a man to be unable to have this ceremony performed over his grave. It would be said, "The dead man has gone with the midrib of the plantain leaf to the grave."

At the time of anointing at the final farewell [the men stood on one side of the body and the women on the other]. (117) The body was unwrapped and the eldest brother washed the face of the dead man with a sponge made of plantain. Then he [washed the face with oil] (117) and dried his hands in the barkcloth wrapping of the body... (Roscoe says on a sponge.)......

If there were no son or grandson to perform this ceremony in the proper fashion other relatives might supply a boy for the occasion, to make the dead seem less of a poor creature.........

When the body had been buried the tomb was covered with dry leaves, and the belts of the gravediggers, as well as the straps which bound the hoes they used to their handles, were left upon the grave..

There were several methods of burial. A common person was merely thrown into the river if he died in the city. If he died away from home the chief of the county in which he died might demand a cow in order to give permission for his burial. [A domestic servant was never buried on the clan burial ground but was merely thrown into the jungle or buried in any convenient place.] (127) People might by special arrangement be buried in the grounds of other clans but in that case trees were not planted at the heads of their graves. Women might be buried any place ......

[Some time after the burial the women were apportioned. Then there was a beer feast and the heads of the heir and of all the women were shaved.] (122) An instrument was played that evening and all the mourners wept.[That night food was prepared for the children and their mothers. Each of them took a small piece] (122) and the rest was trampled under foot. For this meal a type of plantain food usually used only for beer making, was used. This signified that the dead man would never eat or drink of it again.....

There was a song sung at the feast:

> A little mushroom
> I have fallen and remained there
> As a mushroom.

First the men sang it and then the women took part. From then on the weeping was all over until the day that the heir was installed......

When the ceremony of giving the gifts to the heir was over the debtors were all invited to make their claims. Those who didn't do so lost the right to demand them later of the heir. Then the heir and his sister went and cut down a tree or killed a cow to show the wealth of the deceased.

When the successor had been properly installed the clan head gathered all the relatives. After putting aside the share for the heir he distributed the rest among the other people who had taken part in the funeral ceremonies. If the gifts had been given at the installation of the heir of a rich man, most of the important men of the clan received shares even if they had not been present. In the case of the poor men this was not the case and the heir was looked up to by his brothers and sisters as their guardian and major source of livelihood.

In the ceremonies performed for the death of a child no chicken was prepared, a chicken feather was roasted and smelt of instead. For women the sticks used for stringing up a certain type of fish were burnt and the smoke smelt of.

A young child never had a real successor appointed but there was a small ceremony performed somewhat informally. The heir did not sit on the verandah as did the accredited heir of an adult, but he was introduced in the house by the father as the heir. Only for the head of the house was the formal ceremony on the verandah performed. When a child succeeded his brother he was often introduced as the heir of other dead children of the family at the same time....

If a king's servant died without children or other relatives, the king appointed one of the pages to succeed him, giving him half the property and keeping the other half for himself. If it were the servant of a chief who died in this condition, the chief did the same thing for him. The children of a servant became the property of the chief.

There is now a new system of inheritance inaugurated by the native parliament. The body of a chief remains in the house for only a few days and is then buried. The next day the treasurer of the deceased or his widow produces his will and thus are settled the questions of property distribution and the choice of heir. If there is no will, the chief in charge appoints one of the children of the deceased as his heir. If there is no child one of the brothers is appointed. The heir receives a greater share of the property than the other children. The widows and the other relatives are also given some share and the debts of the deceased are paid.

The heir and all the documents are brought before the prime minister who sends them before the king and the parliament. If there are no objections, the king signifies official approval of the affair.

The following afternoon all the participants shave their heads. In the evening they gather to sing hymns to bless the heir. The next morning the clan head dresses the heir in a new barkcloth and presents him to the people. Then he and his sister sit down on barkcloth provided for the purpose and everyone presents them with gifts. The money he uses for the widows and others in need. Following this there is a great feast. The property is then properly divided. The children of the deceased are under the care of the heir, but if he is very young the clan appoints other guardians.

CHAPTER XXII.

GODS AND FORTUNE TELLERS.

Mister Death at Tanda. Nakabale, who was Eŋgeye or the chief priest-landlord at Tanda, and whose great-grandfather lived during Kintu's reign, explained his priesthood in the following manner.

"My forefather told me that that quagmire known as Mr. Death was worshipped by a king. He offered a sacrifice of nine cows, nine goats, sheep and servants, and nine chickens. These offerings he sent through Katale, son of Kaira, of the Mbogo clan. They were brought before Nakabale, who went with the king's messenger to offer these to Mr. Death. When they reached him, Nakabale said "Here are the offerings from the king to you. If anything has angered you, let this calm your majesty."

All these quagmires were supposed to have been dug by Walumbe. Mr. Death is supposed to have been the brother of Nambi Nantu- tululu, the wife of Kintu. The story is told that Mr. Death never died. After quarreling with his brother Kintu and destroying all his offspring he went down into one of these quagmires and stayed there alive. When the Ŋgeye clan found out what had happened Kasudju the chairman of the clan appointed his own son Nakabale to guard the quagmire where Mr. Death was supposed to have gone

down..... All that was really known about these quagmires was
that suddenly a new one appeared.... The place where Mr. Death
was lost was known as Masiro just like the king's burial places.....
When people in the course of an illness became unconscious, it was
thought that Mr. Death was about to take them to his abode.

Waŋga, [at Budu in Sese]. (313) He was the son of Bukulu,
who was supposed to have come with Kintu. [Lubobi was the chief
priest who looked after the temple.] God Waŋga was supposed to
have introduced the art of making walking or fighting sticks. At
one time he got hold of Kusoma of the Lugave clan, who had a son
named Kalali. Kalali had just become the page of Mutebi. It
happened that at this time certain chiefs had gotten to be so
honored and feared that they were thought of as equals of the king.
The king did not like this and angrily determined to put an end to it.
These chiefs were Mande of the Ŋkima clan, at Kabembe, and
Kadjubi of the Nsenene clan at Budjubi. While contemplating
depriving these men of their positions, Mutebi sent his page Kalali
to inquire of Waŋga as to his prediction in this matter..... Waŋga
advised him to get several long sticks and tie cowry shells on them;
then to take several young boys with leaves tied around their necks
and attack the enemy. Kalali left and did just as he was told. First
he attacked Mande. He took the young boys and merely had them
point their long sticks at the enemy. In the same manner Kadjubi
was brought to submission. When Kalali had conquered these two
powerful and dignified chiefs, he asked the king for a permanent
place where the boys could settle. Nsagu in Busiro was granted him
and there the boys settled and became the Royal Fighters. Their
hobby was to make more sticks. Wherever they went they had
only to point the sticks and demand money or cowry shells and it
was granted them. While they were demanding the money they
would knock the sticks on the ground and sing. Any one who refused
to give them money they cursed. During the reign of Mutesa the
people began to refuse to give them anything. When they knocked
and sang the houseowner would make no response, and after they
had gone he would pour water into the holes their knocking left
and say, "Your sins have followed you." This was symbolic of
their washing off any blame. In this way the association was
brought to an end.....

Musisi, [the third son of Bukulu.] (313) He had two [temples,]
Bufuma at Busudju, of which Kafuma of the Nyonyi clan was the
priest, and Funve [at Sese,] of which Maso, Sekema, and Semi-
rembe of the Ŋkima clan were priests. [He was the earthquake god.]
(313)..... His priests shook their bodies as he was supposed to

8

shake his...... A person who trembled in this way from disease
was asked if he was praying to Musisi.

[*Wamala*, the first son of Musisi] in Siŋgo county, tended by
Lusundo of the Nvuma clan', and Mudjumbula of the Fumbe clan...
[He got conjunctivitis from ashes flung in his face by his brother] (314)
and now people who have this disease say, "Wamala is itching me"..
[Lake Wamala was brought about by the breaking of a water jug
he carried.] (314)..... Later, it grew much larger and seemed in
danger of running over into the Katoŋga river and returning whence
it came. He became upset and went to Kidondolima for advice.
This doctor gave him a medicine to pour into the Kibimba river.
This ran into the other. When he poured the medicine into it it ran
into the lake instead......

Wanema, the second son of Musisi. His temple was at Bukasa in
Sese. Muwonda, Sekirita, and Mulegeya, of the Nvuma clan were the
priests. They were responsible for all the religious ceremonies that
took place.

[*Serwaŋga Mukasa*, the first son of Wanema. His temple was at
Bukasa in Sese. Semagumba, Gugu, Sebandide, of the Bugeme clan
were the priests.....] (293) [During the time of the rebuilding of
his house the king sent Gabuŋga] and Namukoka of the Mamba
clan, Kawuŋgu and Muwundakalevu of the Fumbe clan, and
Nakasese the king's uncle. [They took with them as offerings nine
fresh reeds] (292) with their roots, nine wives, nine servants, nine
cows, and nine hundred cowry shells. [The roots cut off the reeds
were to fix the altar. They were also mixed with those others that
made the outer porch.] The king's successor did not have to rebuild
the temple but he was required to double the gifts, which were
presented with a prayer for the blessing of his administration. The
temple was built every alternate reign.

[*Mukasa* was the chief of all the gods.] (290) When the time of his
ceremonies approached a warning was issued by his priests enjoining abstinence on all for a period of four days. Then the priests
went to Musove Harbour to prepare for the ceremony. The head
wife of the high priest, Semagumba, opened the services by digging
a clump of dirt, and all the worshippers followed suit. Several roads
were built — one from the harbour to the temple; Butundu;
Mulwaŋga; Zibika; Ŋkumbalu; Mwesera; Musonzi. All then returned
to the temple and there met Sekayoŋga of the Ŋkima clan, a Bunyama district chief. He built two big houses — Kuma and Tulo —
and eighteen small ones. This completed the first part of the ceremony. Semagumba then tied a cow in Kogero, which was built by
three priests. The priests stripped the bark of several plantain

trees and made a gutter from the temple to the harbor. Two or
more young men were detailed to seize the cows one at a time and
to hold them down while Gugu cut their necks and Semagumba
directed the blood into the gutter that it might flow down into the
lake. Everyone, even the priests, was on that day prohibited from
going on or even near the lake, on pain of death. When all the cows
but one had been executed in this fashion, the priests killed this
last one without ány assistance, spraying the blood from it on the
surrounding buildings. The meat of the others was distributed
among the followers, but this one was the property solely of the
priests, and might be shared only by members of their families and
clans. However, Semukade who had the job of gathering the leaves
on which the meat was prepared, was also privileged to share that
of· the priests, although he was of another clan...........

[After a new temple had been built.....] Semagumba, the head
priest, was left in charge, to guard the god, which was a very large
hammer. Twice a month he entered the temple to be sure that the
hammer had not rusted or had any other ill befall it.

[When people went to Mukasa for an oracle,] Gabuŋga left the
people at Bunyama island and went to Funve to Lubale Musisi's
place to inform him of what was toward. He had to give his sanction
to the undertaking, saying that whatever Mukasa might warn them,
of that he too would warn them. This was because Musisi was
the elder brother.

The people who arrived at the temple were seated in straight
lines, while the prophet entered the house Sikirabaŋga. Inside this
was a curtain dividing it into two parts. The prophet from the inner
one gave to the king's messenger a prophecy which he might take
back to the king.

[Mukasa's prophet was a woman,] (297) Nakaŋgu, of the Mamba
clan. During her prophesying she recited the following chant:

"God, God, the great, come today and help me to judge."
Then the multitude took up the shout and drums were beaten,
After quiet had been re-established she would begin her prophesy.
The belief was that Mukasa had spoken out in the air. [When the
people entered the temple they heard the voice in the air or behind
the curtain.....] (298)

[His priests wore their ceremonial robes throughout the ceremonies.]

[The drums belonging to this god were of special trees.] (296)
For instance the sticks were made of olufugo (Roscoe says they
were made of human bones.) [The head drum was called Beto-
baŋga,] then Nabirye, [then Nabikono..... and fourthly Kikasa.

8*

[There were also ten smaller ones. Kikasa was the first drum to be sounded, and all the others followed it......]

Mukasa was supposed to be very good and kind, and considered everybody his child, never killing anyone. Whenever he came around all the prisoners on his estates were set free. Whenever a priest committed an offense for which he was to be killed Mukasa offered a bull in his stead and this was taken to the outskirts of the place and killed.

The head priest at his death was buried in Bugugu county, Gugu in Kalongo county and Sebandide in Ŋkose country.

[Mukasa had three wives, Nalwaŋga of the Nyonyi clan,] mother of Lwaŋga and Musozi; [Nadjemba of the Ŋoŋge clan,] mother of Buguŋgu and Kisituka; [and Naku of the Fumbe clan who was the mother of Kaumpuli, Nairuma, and Nanziri. These women and their children all became lubale or gods after their death......]

A story is told of how Mukasa came to the capital to prophesy for King Semakokiro, who was suffering with indigestion and had sent for the god. The latter told him to get hold of the indigestion in his stomach and to cure himself. Failing to understand the meaning of this he sent everyone away that he might have a private session with the god. Then he was advised by the god that if he wanted to live long and have a peaceful reign, he must put all his sons in jail. The king did this and also had some of them killed......

When King Mukabya Mutesa became sick he sent Gabuŋga Kaya and Sabaganzi Lubuzi to Sese island to invite Mukasa to give an oracle for the king. The god sailed and arrived at Mutundwe hill after four days. Here he found four houses ready for himself and for his colleagues. These were built by the servants known as Ekikasa and were for Mukasa, Musisi, Sese and Kibuka. The next day these four gods arrived at the palace of the king at Kikandwe.

Before giving his prophecy, Mukasa demanded that the court should retire so that the king might attend him in private. Only the other three gods, some very important chiefs, and the three priests of Mukasa remained. Then Mukasa demanded ninety women, ninety slaves, ninety cows and nine hundred cowry shells. The king refused to do this and the god, very angry, refused to prophesy. After that Mukasa would never go to tell the fortune of a king.....
There must have been some sort of understanding among the gods because they often gave identical prophesies......

[*Kibuka*, the second son of Wanema.] (301) His home was at Mbale in the Mawokota country. Lwomwa, Kituma, Nakantanda-gira, Nakabaŋgo, and Buvi, were his priests......

After the death of Kibuka a wise man arose, Muziŋgu of the

Mamba clan. He dreamed that Kibuka spoke to him and told him they would not bury him. He commissioned him to speak for him, telling him to invade Bunyoro. The next day Muziŋgu prophesied for Kibuka, speaking in his voice. For this reason Mulondo, the king, was very fond of him.

Muziŋgu's first act was to fight those Bunyoro who had invaded Buganda and settled there. After this war the citizens at Mbale buried the body of their hero Kibuka, laying it in the house wrapped in leopard, lion, and hyena skins. During the lifetime of Muziŋgu he was always consulted and his advise followed with reference to any warfare.

[Kibuka's temple] was called Bugya-bukula[1], which means, "old age may bring honor or shame." The other house was Bagamba Munyoro, implying that any Munyoro is excluded from Mbale. Any one who went there was immediately executed, because his countrymen were held responsible for the death of Kibuka. The Baganda coined this proverb: "I am a Muganda of Mbale".....
[There was a third house, Namirembe, in which the prisoners to be killed were kept.] The slaughter place was known as Mpumude which means "I have rested", as it was named by the prisoners who came there to have their lives ended......

The main temple was built seasonally. The king sent eighteen reeds and a bull through Katata of Mabaŋga. The bull was to be killed and its skin cut in strips to make the crown of the house. The official beginning of the house was taken care of by Nakatandagira Sabawali, who initiated the roof-building...... [Immediately several arrests were made. In the afternoon when the house was completed the king sent additional prisoners and those who had already been seized to Mpumude where they were to be executed in order that the granting of a blessing or curse, as desired, might be effected..... When the prisoners had all been killed Kaima was sent to Bunyoro with a log.] (304—306)

Mudjaguzo, Kibuka's royal drums, were named Naku and Kababembe. This latter one was always given to the diviner to use during a war campaign. A third drum Nalubale remained there all the time.

Kibuka appeared in public every month. (Roscoe says only at the time of the building of a new temple for him.) [When the time came the curtains were thrown open and the covers all removed except the leopard, lion, and hyena skins. Then the assemblage was all invited in. There were special seats reserved for the chiefs.] Lwomwa of the Ndiga clan, Prime Minister, was at the right. Nansumbi, Sabadu, of the Fumbe clan, was in the middle.

---

[1] lit., little things develop and grow.

These were the ladies-in-waiting:

Nagalemede	Mamba clan, daughter of Mbadja
Nakitabadja	Mamba clan daughter of Kitabadja
Nalunga	Nvuma clan
Namulondo	Butiko clan
Nansambu	Musoga tribe
Nakaiza	Musoga tribe
Nakabugo	Mbogo clan
Kanyikuli	Ŋgeye clan
Mulopi	Ndiga clan

Next to the ladies-in-waiting were seated:

Buvi	Kasudju, Ndiga clan
Kanyoro	assistant Sabadju
Nansera	assistant Kasudju
Namunene	whose duty it was to cut the log for the main door-step
Kiguli	guardian of Kibuka's second twin, Kalaŋgwa
Kazimba	washer of Kibuka
Sebawutu	barkcloth maker
Kazina	Omusoloza
Namunyi	the thatcher.

On the left hand side of the house were seated:

Nakabaŋgo,	Sabagabo, Fumbe clan, carrier of the god's shield and weapons
Kituma	Omukoŋgozi, Ndiga clan.
Nakatandagira	Sabawali, Ndiga clan
Sabatem	Omubika, Kibuka's nurse, who had to cover him
Kasomba	Kibuka's custom officer
Ŋkunyi	who had to rub Kibuka's skins when they were wet
Kiyaga	who had to get the walls for the temple from Sese island where Wanema, the father of the god, had them ready.
Seruti	Omukamula or squeezer
Walubwa	Sebalidja
Kasambandege	Omugundju, entrusted with the arrow that killed Kibuka
Balikumwa	entrusted with an arrow Kitonyawagulu
Nsimbi	guard of the god's elder twin.

When these had taken their seats the crowd was invited to take the back seats which remained, until the whole yard was filled up. These were the names of the prophets.

Muziŋgu	Mamba clan
Kayandja	Ŋkima clan
Kaindja	Fumbe clan
Nadjambubu	Nyonyi clan
Kiwanuka	Nyonyi clan
Seruyombya	Lugave clan
Kabugo	Mbogo clan
Kirideyo	Kobe clan
Kibaya	Kobe clan
Kikambi	Nsenene clan
Namube	Ŋgeye clan
Nakaŋgu	Ŋgo clan

These prophets were all seated in one row next to the chiefs. They were distinguished from the rest of the crowd by their priestly robes. All priests were clad in barkcloth fastened with two knots. They wore goat skins about their waists and the heads of leopard skins hanging on their backs. In their hands each held the tail of a cow.

[When such an assemblage was held in time of war a priest inspired by Kibuka announced war tactics and these were outlined to the king's general next day......]

[Many of the diviners in the service of Kibuka received messages elsewhere but the more important ones served only at the temple.] At the main temple only aristocrats had their fortunes divined. Only chiefs and the king could meet the obligations imposed by the priests here. Until 1889 Kibuka and his prophets were regarded with esteem. But during the second reign of Mwaŋga, Kibuka's power was swept aside and these things were temporarily abolished. Kibuka seems to have been regarded as a temporal king as well as a god. He was particularly respected in Kaima's county. When the latter went to worship before him though he might be called away by the king himself, he might not go unless the god granted him permission to leave. All Kibuka's seats were called Namulondo just as were the king's.

The story goes that his body was never buried. I inquired of the Mbale chiefs and was told that a body of Christians headed by one Serwano Maziŋga (Mukitagobwa country) who was also captain of several battalions of the army, took the supposed body of Kibuka and threw it by the wayside, when the warriors were anxious to get for their wear the skins in which it was wrapped. These warriors said that nothing was inside these wrappings but a long dried piece of meat. I think that the Mbale chiefs buried him secretly and then deceived the others by announcing that he did not want to be buried.

They did this to gain prestige before the king..... Or they may have taken and hidden it later.......

[*Nende*, the son of Mukasa whose temple was Bukerere in Kyagwe. county. Wanzu of the Ŋkima clan and Kadjugudjwe of the Butiko clan were his priests. He was very well esteemed and had a large following...... His enclosure had only one gate.] (308) It was in Siganira[1] house. This word refers to sexual relations, and implies, "I approve of the women of Nende."

Nende had two main buildings, Buntubiza and Kigudo. When one was under construction he moved to the other. In the former there was a mat in the center of the floor on which the diviner sat with a heavy stick about a foot and a half long. It was called Ŋkono. Whenever the diviner gave utterance, he struck the threshold. Nende drank no intoxicating beverages, but used only coffee grains and mpande.[2]

[These were the ladies who were always seated behind Nende:]

Nakirwade was the most loved. To show this he used to swear by her name saying, "I am the husband of Nakirwade." Then the drummers and trumpeters would sound in high praise, saying, "Lenda! Lenda!"

[Nabweteme,] Zansanze, Lugogo, [Nagadya,] (308) Nanyoŋga, and Nabitakuli. These Nakirwade regarded as her wives, as an expression of love and security.

The representative of a king or a war general who was sent to the temple was regarded as the brother-in-law of Nende.

This was the explanation given of this custom..... When Semakokiro was a prince at Namwezi, Nende foretold that he was soon to be king. He promised to give the god one of his children, and he fulfilled his vow when he ascended the throne. He gave to Nende his daughter Nabweteme, and several others followed her.

On his right were seated Wanzu, Waŋgobagoba, Bukuŋkumuse, Mukaya, Kabalaba, and Kalimi, and then the whole crowd.

On one side of the mat were seated Nyoŋge and Kabona. Beyond the mat were Kadjugudjwe, Nalukade, and Sebwato, Namiŋgo, and Taketa. Others were seated according to the remaining space. Kalabalaba, the king's uncle, was seated in the center ever since the reign of Semakokiro. Before he started the war against his brother he went to Nende to have a prognostication. No one present was allowed to tell Djundju that his brother was plotting against him. After Semakokiro had gained the throne he appointed a representative to stay and watch the proceedings.

---

[1] lit., I do not refuse.　　　　　[2] a kind of vegetable.

[Nende was brought out to the public every two and half years.] (308) At this time he was clad in new barkcloth and seated on fresh barkcloths, lion and leopard skins. The god looked just like a native instrument called Eŋgalabi. It was wound round with several types of beads, and had a hollow and a large head at one head. Parrot feathers and colobus monkey fur were put at the head. At the other end the stick had a long point which was stuck into the ground to make the god stánd. This gave Nende the nickname of the one-legged god. On account of this his diviners used to hop about on one leg. They also left a patch of hair on their shaven heads and wore their robes with the two knots characteristic of priests. They wore goat skins about their waists.

[His ceremonies lasted for nine days, during which he was brought out every day.] He was also, at other times, to be seen inside the temple wrapped in several barkcloths. The assemblage which came to do him honor was known as Lwanyo. During the time of the ceremonies, drums like those of the king were beaten. Galinya was beaten every day, and any general who represented Nende in a campaign was given this drum to use. Basege and several small drums were also beaten, like the royal drum Mudjaguzo. The drums were beaten in a large wide courtyard, surrounded by several buildings. The main building, Buntubiza, faced west. There was not as great a wealth of custom about this god as about some of the others. Nende never ordered anyone arrested or killed, and the ceremonies were all peaceful and quiet.

[*Mirim*, the son of Mukasa.] His temple was in Buswa on Sese. His only priest was Muwonda. (Roscoe says he had only priestesses.) [Mirim went to the front himself in time of war. He would go into the camp of the enemy at night and steal a warrior's spear] (314) and bring it back saying, "Here is an enemy's weapon. I give it to you as a sign that you will win the battle tomorrow." If he failed to steal anything, the warriors were all very much depressed and were therefore easily defeated.

[*Kaumpuli*,] (310) whose temple was at Buyego in Bulemezi. [Kanalira of the Fumbe clan was the priest. Naku, the wife of Kayemba, was his mother. When he was born he lacked both arms and legs.] (307) If a person had swollen glands it was said that this god had done it. His name itself means plague. There is still a great deal of fear of this plague from which many die. After the population had been thus ravaged, Kaumpuli spoke to the survivors, "Come! Now I have forgiven you and I will take you back to your homes." Then he went to his own country place and made a great deal of beer. This he drank until he became drunk. He went through the villages giving blessings and speaking kindly to the peasants. He told them that the enemy had been conquered and they might once more start planting. The people believed him and paid him everything he demanded.

[*Nagawonyi* whose temple was at Banda in Bulemezi county. God (Roscoe says goddess) of the harvest......] (315)

[*Nagadya*, goddess,] whose headquarters were at Ŋkumba village [in Busiro.] (318) Her temple was called Bulam and her priest Fulu.

[*Nalwoga*, also female, with headquarters at Nsazi in Sese.]

[*Kiwanuka* was god of the thunder bolt and the lightning. His home was Buwanuka hill in Busiro county.]

[*Namalele* wore several animal skins. When about to prophesy he beat his head mercilessly with a stick. His temple was in Kyagwe county.] (317)

Ndaula Kawali had a temple on Mubende hill in Buwekula.

[*Duŋgu* was called the King's Beast. [He was the patron of the hunters] (311) and had a temple at Mabira in Kyagwe.

[*Katonda*] (312) had a temple at Butonda in Kyagwe.

Nabuzana ⎫
Mudjobe ⎬ All had priestesses for attendants.
Kagole ⎭

Mukwaŋga's temple was at Nseke in Mawokota.

Nabagasere was the interpreter of the king's riddles.

The following gods were all on islands:

Lumfuwa	Kome island
Kisigula	,,
Masoŋga	Djana
Semafum	Bubeke
Mpumula	,,
Lwuŋgu	,,
Sekundi	,,
Lwaŋga	,,
Damulira	,,
Nanvuma	Bukasa
Damba	,,
Buwaŋga	,,
Kyato	,,
Sekitende	,,
Bugoŋga	,,
Simba	,,
Ŋkose	Maziŋga
Bundjazi	Bundjazi

Nsaŋgi	Serinya
Ŋgoma	Bukasa
Kyaŋga	Bugala
Baŋga	,,
Kibaŋga	,,
Kinyamira	,,
Lutaboka	,,
Kyabuima	,,
Ŋkubandjeru	Bubembe
Buguŋgu	,,
Mwesera	,,
Bukuku	,,
Wada	,,
Bugana	Bugana
Nambubi	Kibibi
Haŋga	Buvu
Sese	Buniŋga
Semugandja	Bufumira
Kabale	Kitabo
Buyovu	Buyovu

Kaindu was a tree at Kiwambya in Bulemezi which prophesied.

Kitenda was a crocodile near Damba Island in Sese to which prisoners were fed.

Mayandja was a river at Seguku in Kyadondo, which gave oracles.

[Sezibwa was a river in Kyagwe county] (318) which prophesied.

Kawenda in Mawokota, Lwamirindi in Bulemezi, Nawandege in Mawokota, were also rivers of note in this connection.

[Mbadjwe, snake. Temple in Butambala county, whose priest was the county chief.] (327)

Sali, a stone, in Lake Nalubale near Bundjako on the Ŋkima clan lands. The children born there are all named Sali.

Kisozi, a hill in Gomba county, the chief land of the Nsenene clan.

Nakalaŋga, a forest in Kyagwe which also prophesied. In this forest there were small parasitic insects which the natives called "small dogs" which sucked the blood so as to reduce the victim to a mere skeleton. They became pigmies, but had strong powerful voices. They were called Nakalaŋga, and could never have children. (cp. p. 163)

Mubiru, also a Kyagwe forest.

[Some high hills were homes of the gods and also sources of prophesy.] (319) Bowa, [Sempa, Walusi], Katerandulu, Kigozi, Busowa, were all in Bulemezi. [These were sanctuaries to the people in time of siege, as they might be used only for worship, and anyone violating this was in jeopardy, though he might be the king's representative.] There were also sacred hills in Siŋgo county — Mubende, Magala, Kagaba, Bulondo, Bwandja, where the royal drums were cut; in Mawokota, there were Sabwe, Kisitu, and Mpaŋga as places of refuge. In Gomba, Sagesi, Kisozi; in Kyadondo, Ntinda and Kuŋgu; in Busiro, Baka; in Kyagwe, Wagala and Buvuma. Some of these were forests, most hills. There were also some minor sacred places which were also sanctuaries. There was also a village in Busiro called Maya, belonging to chief Sebukoko, where one was equally free from arrest.

The so-called gods were formerly human beings. Their attendants imitated their voices and claimed to be inspired by them. The priests who attended the temple and gave out the prophecies were highly revered, sometimes more than the gods they represented. Before this system was introduced the prophesying was done with sandals. Afterwards anyone could get wealthy by pretending to represent a hill, forest, etc. Despite the influence of Christianity and education, the system is not yet all gone.

[This was the procedure used to cure the king when he was ill.] (342) A cow and a goat were killed at the palace door. The doors, window sills, and so forth, were then sprinkled with the blood. Grass known as olweza and bombo was tied to Mulemberembe, Mulamula and Kadjolyendjovu, and painted with the blood. These were then laid in the doorway and covered and the king made to jump over them. The god said that this washed the king of all his iniquities. The grasses used were symbolic, the olweza of prosperity, and the bombo of the supreme power of the king. Mulemberembe meant that the king might stroll about the county and think of the problems of state. Mulamula meant that the king was just in his judgments, and Kadjolyendjovu was a symbol of power and honor for the king, "like that of an elephant towering in the jungle".

[The gods, and those who prophesied with leather, chickens, water, etc. used practically the same methods. A plantain tree was split into two parts and then put in front of a house door, supported by two men.] The king with a spear [would then pass through it.] The spear and [his barkcloths were left on the tree and he re-entered the house naked. The sections of the plantain tree were then cast upon the crowded section of a road and there pierced with reeds. In this way the disease was handed on to a chance passer. This was known as okunabula, to strip of bad spirits. Chiefs and even peasants were also treated in this fashion.] (343)

It was forbidden for a prisoner to be taken through the following

courtyards with a rope about his neck. He had to be untied and
passed through them as a free man. If the guard did not allow this
his prisoner might be helped to escape him, and he would be fined.
On the other hand if a prisoner escaped and entered one of these
houses he was considered to have gained his freedom and might
not be re-arrested.

Kaŋgawo's	in Bulemezi
Seŋgoba	at Kiti in Kyadondo
Muwemba's	at Musebe, in Siŋgo
Sabaganzi's	at Kodja in Kyagwe
Muwaŋga	at Kiwaŋga
Kawuta	at Nyeŋga
Kabwege's	at Busiro
Makamba's	at Budo
Gabuŋga's	at Djuŋgo
Mutawulira	at Butaulira in Butambala

These courtyards were known as social benevolent courts.

[Prognostication by means of a sandal. When a person came to such
a soothsayer he would bring out nine shoes.] (338) The ninth,
decorated with cowry shells and other things, was known as Naka-
bambagiza[1], which meant "the shoe that rules the other eight". They
were all placed in a line and then the fortune-teller sat on one side of
the door and the seeker in the rear corner of the house. Nine cowry
shells and a vertebra were then produced and a [ten by five foot
cowskin spread on the floor. The fortune-teller then advised,] (338)
suggesting an offering of beer to the gods and ancestors, and a goat,
chicken, and barkcloth as an offering for the patient, if anyone was
sick. [If these effected a cure, a reward was given to the fortune
teller.] (339) (R. has not shoes, but strips of leather.)

The suppliant would do as he had been bidden. He would make
beer and build a special temple for the gods. Then he would bring
the sick person near and begin to pray. "O Kibuka, Wanema,
Mukasa, Mirim, Muwaŋga, and all the ghosts of my forefathers,
and also those of the gods whose names I have forgotten to call at
this hour, who have not forgotten me. Guard his majesty; Lubuga,
the queen mother; Katikiro; that they may all live long and peaceful
lives. I am therefore offering to you this chicken, goat, and barkcloth." A chicken feather and a small piece of goat skin and barkcloth were used in place of the actual offerings because the temple was
small and for private use only. At the end of this prayer he poured
beer on the ground and said, "Have mercy upon this sick person."

[1] lit., the loud-mouthed one.

If a sick person was cured, he carried a jar of beer to the sooth-sayer, to whom the original seeker introduced him, saying, "He is your servant, he has come and brought gifts as an offering for your blessing which restored him to life."

[Prognostication by means of a chicken.] (370) The person who was making the inquiries had to supply some of his saliva in a small jug. This the fortune teller poured into the mouth of a chicken before killing it. He took out the insides and dipped them in water. Then he [examined the entrails very thoroughly. From his findings he gave his reading.] (340) There were three or four eŋkebes. If there were three it meant that the sick person would eventually get well. Four meant the opposite. If a man were seeking a chiefly position four eŋkebes was the lucky sign. The eŋkebes were groups of meat in the intestines.

[Divination by water. The diviner gathered herbs] known as ebiŋgabazim. [These were ground and put on a stone over which the priest poured the liquid from a jug into which the fortune-seeker had urinated. If this scattered the medicine evenly there was no cause for fear. If it was scattered in odd directions, this meant death.] (341) (Roscoe has the opposite.) If this occurred the diviner advised his client to make an offering to the gods that it might die instead and he be saved. This sort of diviner was known as "A dried and powdered leaves of a tree diviner," or Mukyula.

Divining with eŋkisa. The diviner cut five two or three inch long sticks and put them in a basket or clay pot full of water. The fortune was favorable if the five sticks stayed together, but unfavorable if one of them separated. This too meant death.

[Ebyonzira — the offering of something accursed. There were two divisions of these. One was that of scapegoats in the case of an illness on the part of the king. The objects designated (as in Roscoe) were taken to Bunyoro and there set free.] (324) The group in charge of this then proceeded to loot the Bunyoro villages and divide the spoil. Some of it was set aside as an offering to the gods. These objects were also constantly being killed about the palace gates and near the king's dwelling, and places where he frequently visited. Chiefs also condemned cows and goats as scapes, but only the king included human beings in the lot........

[The following were the greatest "horns" and were nationally respected.] Some of them were fixed in the horns of cows or buffaloes. Others were in long jars or in the horns of rhinoceroses. They were used exclusively by the wealthy priests and diviners.

[Kizuzi Namuzinda
Nambaga

Lukeŋge
Nakavuma
Nakaŋgu
Kibaziŋga
Baisemugwaŋga
Sekabemba
Kasadja,] (323) and many others.

When evening came, the fires were put out in the houses
in which the services connected with these fetishes were to take
place. The owner then started rattle music. The whole assemblage
joined, while drinking beer. When the music became fascinating the
fortune-teller spoke very loudly through his long hollow stick. This
was supposed to be the voice of the horn.

[Capturing of ghosts. This was done when people were sick. The
ghost catchers used one of their party to catch the ghost of the sick
person.] (19) They sang songs and the man on the floor began to cry
and to utter phrases depicting the ghost. "Why are you after me ?
Why do you want to kill me ? I had better run away from here,"
he would cry. When the ghosts seized him the others would clap a
large flat jar over his mouth. He would say, "Ghosts, come out
of my friend and enter the jar." He then would vomit into the jar,
continuing to protest his innocence of any offense. Then the fortune-
teller tied a leaf without a hole over the mouth of the jar. "Since you
have killed people all these days I have captured you," he said.

There was another method of curing those possessed by ghosts.
The fortune-teller who was summoned covered the sick person with
barkcloth and spoke in a strange tone. [He took a pipe and blew
the smoke upon the sick man.] (101) He had some charms in a
gall-bladder. These he squeezed so that they made a sound. He
also brought two large jars, in which he put some dry grass and
water. Then he set the jars on two smoked leaves and standing by
the soothsayer he would squeeze the bladder and ask, "Why did you
come to harm our friend ? Come into these jars and I will give you
water to drink." He would make noise with the bladder and put it
into the jar. Then he burst it and said, "Get hold of the murderer. He
has entered into the jar." Then men tied the jars, which were burnt
to ashes the next day. Meanwhile a medicine was given to the sick
man, which he vomited if a cure had been effected .... The fortune-teller was then paid everything he demanded.

Kizuzi. These were the king's horns which helped to reveal
thieves, murderers, adulterers, and so on. One of the keepers was
the priest, and he spoke in a small voice advising as to what was to

be done. The keepers became wealthy because they were allowed to confiscate the property of those who fell under their suspicion. Often they seized the persons as well.

A luck medicine, Kisuwa, was made of herbs and tobacco leaves. Everyone from peasant to king mixed these. A chief going to court would drink some of it saying, "I don't want anyone speaking ill of me or anything wrong to happen. I want to walk a free man, safe from any harm." Should he return home safe or promoted to a new office, he would attribute this to the efficacy of this medicine.....
Those who did not know how to mix this bought it from a specialist. It was drunk on the right side of the porch, while kneeling.

Okulumika. To bleed by cupping. This was done by the diviners. One would come to a very sick person and say that he was being charmed; that he would work a cure at the price of a goat. If the family consented, he would make some little clay horns into which he mixed a few hairs. When he was ready to cup the sick person he would put one of them under his tongue, but he would cough and open his mouth to show the people that there was nothing in it. Then he would make several cuts with a razor, and prepare his cowhorn cup with a soft smoked leaf which he placed about the edge. He would chew some medicine and spit it into the cup, at the same time letting the little clay horn slip into it. Then he put the cup against the place where he had cut, and sucked it hard so that it would stick. He smoked a pipe, after which it was time to remove the cup. He prepared some fine leaves and taking off the cup, he poured the blood in it over the leaves. He then showed the people, who were all about, what had been killing their friend. They examined the blood and finding the hair thought that the horn had come from his body and he was now cured.

However there were and still are real doctors who cured diseases through the administration of medicines. If these failed they would admit it so that another might cure. They were able to cure leprosy, but only in its early stages. There was a salivary disease known as Kalusu which they were not able to cure, and spasms were baffling to them. [Cupping is still resorted to,] (99) particularly by the women for headaches.

CHAPTER XXIII.
JUDICIAL PROCEDURE.

[A plaintiff who was robbed or cheated went to court with twenty-two cowry shells and started a suit.] (260) The cowry shells were known as eŋkanam. Before they were introduced a goat

skin was used. This word means goatskin. [The court then sent for
the defendant. After both sides had pleaded their cases in a first
hearing, the chief demanded a preliminary fine of a goat and a barkcloth apiece:] (260) If the pre-fine was not paid immediately, decision
was suspended for a few days so that it might be collected. The
chief then reviewed the case of each side, inquiring as to whether
he was doing it right. Then he rendered his verdict. [The guilty
person was expected to pay a fine and costs. If he refused to accept
the guilt and desired to appeal, he refused to pay this and appealed
to a higher court.] (361) Here he accused the chief of having found
him guilty without sufficient evidence. The chief was then called
and a hearing granted.

[There was also the court of the Katikiro.] (361) This was known
as Gombolola. If the findings of the lower court were upheld here
the defendant might go to the supreme court, that is to the Parliament before the king. [He might appeal to ordeal if the verdict
was still against him. If the king consented he sent him together
with the plaintiff and a messenger to chief Magunda who was the
mixer of the ordeal.] The ordeal-liquor or madudu was made from a
small round fruit, bumpy and very much resembling the colocynth
berry, with wide and shiny leaves. [He ground these fruits, adding a
pint of water. Then he filtered it and divided it into two parts, one
for each. He laid down a dry leaf before them in a straight line and
told each that if he was sure that his cause was just he was to come
forward and give thanks. When they had both become drunk, they
both went forward. The first one to jump over the leaves and give
thanks before Magunda was considered guiltless.] (341) If the
defendant lost again there was nothing for it but to pay the fine.
If the plaintiff lost he had also to pay compensation to the man
whom he had falsely accused.

The ordeal liquor was stronger than an ordinary intoxicant. Some
people who knew themselves to be too easily intoxicated were
sometimes allowed to have friends take the ordeal for them......

If a man accused another of using charms the chief immediately
resorted to the ordeal. If both failed to jump over the leaf, they were
fined a cow, a goat, and a barkcloth, for the trouble.

If a person was robbed, and suspected a certain house of containing the thief, he would demand a messenger from the chief to
search the house. If the goods were not found there he paid a fine
of a cow, a goat, and a barkcloth for the false accusation.

If a man found another committing adultery with his wife, he
confiscated all his property, sharing the spoils with the chief of
the village, who might pay the fine and save the man if he desired to

9

do so. [If the woman at fault was a king's or chief's wife, both the parties were put to death.] If the man was in some way related to the chief, instead of being killed he had his ears cut off and his eyes taken out. (Roscoe says the punishment for adultery is a fine, and maiming.) (261)

If a man cheated his friend and ran off, and they later chanced to meet upon the road, the plaintiff might appeal to a passerby to arrest the offender. Then they would all proceed to the court of the chief of this third party, who called together those of the two others. Then they paid the third party a fee and he turned the case over to them.

When a quarrel between two neighbors developed into a fight and one was struck a hard blow with a stick, and answered it with a spear, the man who had really been wounded automatically won the case. If the retaliation was in like coin, the man who had struck the first blow was judged guilty.

If a traveler forced a woman to give him food, and a battle ensued when the villagers came to her aid, the responsibility rested with the woman, should one of the travelers be speared. It was not considered wrong for travelers to help themselves to ready-to-eat food. The woman would be given to them as a maid servant. Should one of the travelers, using his spear even in self-defense, kill a villager, he was guilty of murder. He was delivered over to the people and killed. A traveler might invite himself to meals, and in time of plenty, pick as many bananas as he liked without permission.

[Two parties might not conduct a sale without the presence of a third as witness,] (452—456) who had to be given a share of the proceeds, or endobolo. The tax for selling a woman was one female goat, for a servant one male goat, fifty cowries for a cow, and five for a goat. During the reign of Suna, the sale of a cow was fined 100, of a goat 50 shells. (These are not the same as ten percent by Roscoe's prices. He says sales were at regular markets.) (452—456)

The tax on a second hand article served as a guarantee to the purchaser that he was getting an honestly acquired article. This was not necessary for an article which was sold where it was made, so that its origin could easily be proven. It also served as a protection against thieves, as anybody could produce a witness of the acquisition of any article he had come by honestly. If a man was arrested as a suspect his supposed witness was sent for. When he arrived he showed sixty cowry shells — the equivalent of a cow — to the court. Before the accused he announced that he had received payment as witness of the sale of the article in question. Then the shells were returned to him. Should the witness fail to respond in this fashion, guilt was assumed on the part of the accused. The chiefs of the plaintiff and of the defendant were both present at the hearing. If the case went against the plaintiff, he was held as a thief since he had attempted to gain possession of something not rightly his. He was fined a cow, a goat, and the costs. The fine he paid to the defendant. His chief might pay for him and then hold him as his property, on the oath of a third party to be responsible for his non-desertion. He remained a servant to the chief until he was able to pay off the debt. The chief of the winner shared by taking a goat as payment for his work. On the other hand the defendant might be proven a thief and in that case he would be made to pay a hundred per cent fine. [In the old days a thief was punished with death.] (264) Today the heavy fine is only a substitute for it. The theft of a woman, particularly a king's wife, is still punished by death. There is a native proverb representing this: "That which has nowhere to go has its finger cut off."

If a person fired his grass, as was customary during the dry season, and if this by accident ignited and destroyed a neighbor's house, the man was held guilty of arson and had to make good all the damages.

A man who sheltered a criminal without himself being aware of the crime when it was committed, was not considered guilty, but he was expected when he knew to send the offender with a "little axe", that is a cow, to the people who had been injured. They might either kill the criminal or enslave him.

If certain men were known to have stolen cattle from a neighboring village, their own chief would raid them, arresting them and killing those who attempted to resist. If the hearing revealed that they were indeed guilty, they were put to death. Otherwise they were freed. They might be saved from death if relatives came to the rescue with presents of young girls, and so forth.

[A person caught robbing the crops at night was immediately speared, and thrown out with the stolen article tied about him, as a warning to passersby.] (15) If the owner of the crops chose, he might merely arrest him and force him to pay a large fine. If a robber proved unable to meet this he was enslaved. The village chief was always entitled to some considerable share of the fine. Should it be a case of enslaving, the owner had himself to pay a forfeit to the thief.

If a woman stole a stone on which a chief's sponges were beaten, she was condemned to enslavement at the place where she stole it. If she were married, her husband paid a fine of a white goat, that she might return home, after returning the stone. The reason for this was that all the sponges for bathing were beaten on these

9*

stones, so that their theft was equivalent to that of the wife who beat them.

If a woman ran away from her husband, any man who found her might report it to the court of the chief. She remained at his home for six months and if by the end of this time she remained unclaimed she automatically became his wife. If her former husband discovered her later there might be a legal contest. If she had born the finder children her former husband had no claim to these. If the woman was found in the house of a man who had not reported to his chief he was sued for illegal marriage. The punishment was confiscation of all his belongings, which went to the husband and the chief. The chief, if he were fond of him, might save him by a large payment. Sometimes the man himself was also seized.

If two herd-boys were fighting, and the eye of one was injured, the other paid him a cow, a goat and a girl. A boy who injured a girl's name had to pay her a cow and a goat.

A man who while drunk broke the center porch pole of another man's house was fined a white goat, a white chicken, and a bead. This was because [this was the main part of the house.] When a house was demolished the owner never used this pole again, not even for firewood, but threw it away. Many ceremonies, such as the giving of clan names to the children, and the chief's morning washing of his face, were performed about this pole.

If a man dug a hole outside his house and covered it with grass, this was announced among the neighbors. After that if a cow fell into the trap it became his property, the owner being entitled to a leg and the chief to part of it. A wild animal thus entrapped had also to be shared with the chief.

A traveling salesman had to give a sample of his wares to the chief of a village to gain the right to market them there. Otherwise he was ordered away and anyone who sheltered him was fined a goat.

If the flocks of a shepherd destroyed the crops of a peasant of the neighborhood, the flocks were confiscated and the shepherd fined a hoe, which when paid redeemed his flocks. If it were not paid for a time and one of his animals was lost or killed by a wild animal, the confiscator was not held responsible.

If a cow charged and killed a cow belonging to another owner, the dead cow became the property of the owner of the killer, and the man whose cow had been killed received the live one in exchange. If a cow trampled a grave which was being watched by relatives of the deceased, the cow was confiscated and held till its owner paid a fine of one goat. If he did not pay the cow might be killed and eaten. If a shepherd deliberately killed an animal that did not belong to his chief, he was accused before a court and had to return a live one to the despoiled flock. If a man borrowed a male goat to use in his flock and it was killed by wild animals, he had to return a ram. If any of these cases came to court, the winner had to pay a hundred cowry shells, a cow, or a goat, according to his ability.

CHAPTER XXIV.

HUNTING CUSTOMS.

All hunters had horns and whistles as part of their equipment. When one of them found the sleeping-place of an animal he sounded one of them to apprise the others of the discovery. They all took their nets and came to the place in silence. When a hunter went out to trail an animal he followed the foot-prints to a thickly grown part of the forest. Here he walked about in a radius of two to four hundred yards. If he found no spoor, he returned to the place where he had lost trace of it and after carefully fixing the spot in his mind he returned to gather his co-hunters. [They encircled the place which should contain the animal with nets suited to the size of it which they could tell by the tracks. Bells were then tied about the hunting dogs] (449) and these were driven in at the exact point where the animal had entered the covert. The leader followed after the dogs, shouting encouragement at them. The hunters who were at the side where there were no nets also joined the shout. [The animal then rushed away from the noise and into the nets, and it was killed as it became entangled,] (449) even though it might be so ferocious and powerful an animal as a leopard or a lion. (Roscoe has the net completely surrounding the district, and also says this method was not used for lions, etc., but only for the ordinary food animals.

[If the hunters were unsuccessful they went to the god Duŋgu to be told more successful methods. If these proved satisfactory, they took a piece of meat to Duŋgu to express their gratitude. This was usually a piece of the back. The skull of a buffalo was also taken to the temple, after the meat had been immediately consumed on the field.] (448) Also a bundle of fire-wood was taken. This was cut from a special tree. A fire was made from this at the temple at which the priest warmed himself. Then he told them to go and hunt; that they would have good luck... (R. says the god is always consulted in advance.).......

Dividing the Spoils.

[The leader was entitled to a leg, the back,] (450) and the skin. [The killer was entitled to a side,] (450) and the second killer was also given a special part. The owner of the dogs was entitled to the chest, and if no dogs had been used those people who had acted as beaters were given this share. [The others divided an arm among themselves.] (444) If a dog was the killer, as of a civet cat, the dog owner was entitled to two legs and an arm.

[The hunting dogs were very carefully attended to. When a man returned from the hunt he fed his dogs first.] (450) If his wife had prepared no food for the dog she was beaten. [The dogs were given two-thirds of the entrails of all the meat taken.] When a chief killed a civet cat he gave his dogs a leg, the neck, and the head. When two were killed the dogs were given a whole one.

CHAPTER XXV.

BLOOD-BROTHERHOOD.

[The oath of blood-brotherhood was considered absolutely binding.] (168)..... (Rite as given in Roscoe, page 19) If a man cheated his blood-brother, the aggrieved one cursed him, and this caused his death. This was the curse used: "Let me die a poverty-stricken man while you my blood-brother who cheated me go about and grow rich." Even the king might never kill a man with whom he had sworn this oath.

When a man cheated his blood-brother and was rebuked for it he prepared to pay him back. He made a meal, at which they both ate. The aggrieved man dipped a piece of banana in goat soup and said to the other, "Take this and eat it. I no longer hold anything against you." The other party did the same thing, saying, "Pray for me to recover from all the curses you put upon me. Here I return all my sins to you." The party at fault also often gave a young relative to the other as a hostage until all the grievances should be adjusted.

This meal had to take place, as before it the aggrieved party refused to have anything to do with the other person, or with his relatives or property. Also he refused to eat any but roasted food, and to shave his head. He would often say, "Let me die in poverty while my blood-brother who cheated me is becoming rich." If the guilty party found that a member of his family became ill, he made inquiries of the gods, and was ordered to return all the property in order that his relative might recover.

If a domestic servant should make this oath with the son of a chief it raised his status to that of the other man.

Of course, there were some people who cheated while taking the oath. For instance, some would spit out the coffee bean instead of swallowing it. Doing this sort of thing often made a man very sick. Their mouths might swell or become twisted, or they might have some other deformity, plainly advertising their trickery. It is said though that no harm would come to those who spat it out without delay. They might turn around and ransack the house of the other because they feared nothing.

[If a person were falsely accused of something, he might swear he had not done it,] by his father, [his mother] (268) or that the heaven and earth might swallow him or the king cut off his head. These oaths were all considered binding.

CHAPTER XXVI.

DRESS.

In the old days Baganda dress consisted of animal skins. The bark-cloth clothes were introduced by a man of the Ŋoŋge clan..] (443)

Skins were prepared for clothing by having the hair rubbed off with sand. This was put inside the skin and the whole worked with a stone to get rid of the fragments of meat left within. [After the skins were dried they were rubbed with butter to soften them] (409) and then they were cut square and sewn together to form a piece as large as a barkcloth. Two pieces were left protuding to serve as knot pieces. This preparation was for the chiefs only. The common people wore the skins with the hair on.

The skins of the cow, hyena, and a small jackal-like animal, were considered good looking and were worn over the barkcloth. Chiefs engaged on business for the king wore these with a belt about them, as a courtesy to the wives of the king, so that they might see the respect in which their husband was held. Those whose duties were with the wives of the king were not allowed to wear such nice costumes, but had to stick to ordinary cowhide.

[Girls wore pieces of wood strung together about their waists, and small varicolored pieces hanging down in front, until they were twelve, when they changed to barkcloth.] (443)

CHAPTER XXVII.

SPORTS AND GAMES.

These games are for the children and also for the adults.

Stick Battle. This game was played chiefly by the king's pages. Fifty played on each side. The results were often almost as serious as though they had used spears instead of sticks. The side that lost most of its fighters by one casualty or another was driven from the scene and considered conquered.

Kicking. [Two groups of pages would challenge each other to a kicking contest. Each side would try to knock down the individuals on the other team by kicking them.] (79) An outstanding feat was to kick one's way out of an encircling group of kickers. This game was only indulged in by those who knew that they were strong. It was a great favorite with shepherds. The game was introduced from Busoga.

Plantain tree game. This game was very popular and was played by the king himself. It was played by hitting at one's opponents with plantain trees. It could cause serious pain.

Ebirumbirumbi (a type of grass root). These were uprooted and used in the game. It was a game which required strength and fortitude. It was very popular with the shepherds. [The king played it with Semanobe at Budo just after his enthronement.] (193)

Riding upon the Bulls. The herders trained their cows to carry them, and sometimes contests on cow-back were arranged between two groups. The visiting team sometimes had to ride for over an hour to the assigned spot. They went there with as many tricks of riding as they could master. The best riders were selected and opposed each other, horning and pushing. The side with the greater number of able fighters won. The services of the cows were recognised in a decoration of dry grass which was placed on each that had performed ably. A similar battle between goats and sheep was also sometimes enjoyed.

Following this there was always a wrestling match between the shepherds. [Wrestling was a favorite sport for all from shepherds to king.] (78) It was always done on a wide level spot, and the kings and his court often attended, the king upon his royal stool, and the chiefs seated upon skins. [Music was played by flutists, drummers, clappers and singers] (78) and at its climax the hero of the day would come forth and dance around until a champion was produced by the challenging team. They walked about together, till one of them stretched out his right hand, bending it about fifteen degrees, when the other did the same. Then they grappled, the superior one lifting his opponent against his back, or tripping him. A score was made by throwing the other player down on his back with his shoulders and elbows touching the ground. Both then knelt before the king and gave thanks. If there was any dispute as to the winner, a desision was made by the chiefs. A man lost and had to sit down if he was thrown twice. If one of the fighters acted amusingly, the king paid attention to him. A wrestler whose fighting was purely defensive was considered cowardly and not a good fighter. The kings not only invited champions to wrestle before them but sometimes themselves took part. Mukabya in particular was fond of wrestling and often wrestled with his brothers.

Stick-rolling. Each player cuts three or more sticks for the game, which may be played by teams or just as a free for all. [The one who could roll his stick farthest started. He laid his stick cross-wise ten or twelve feet away and the others tried to hit it with theirs. The sticks which did not hit it were taken as slaves, and were beaten by the captain, so hard that sometimes they broke in .pieces.] (77) If the same captain played the second time it was called "to better them," and the third time he won he was allowed to beat the sticks into the jungle as far away as he could. He was very jubilant as he watched the others going after their sticks, and taunted them, singing:

"When the stick of your friend has gone astray, oh! astray,
It is the champion who set it wandering.
Oh! astray! I, the champion, shall repay you."

Wheel-Rolling. This game was played by opposing teams and was played in the streets, as was the preceding one. The players stood opposite each other, each holding in his hand a "tangler" . made of two pieces of corncob on a long string. One of the players stood in the middle of the road, rolled the wheel down, and the player on the other side tried to stop it with his tangler. If the end man failed the others tried. A player who stopped it sang out:

"It is all tangled! It is all tangled up!
Spare it for me! Spare it for me!"

Then the team which rolled the wheel came to examine the tangling. The player who had stopped it, when the tangles had been counted, stood where the wheel fell and held it in his outstretched hand. The three or four opponents (depending on the number of times the tanglers were found to be wrapped about the wheel) aimed at it with their tanglers. Those throws which succeeded made their throwers free, but the others were taken as servants by the opposing team and made to sweep the courts, where the wheels and tanglers were prepared.

The game continued with the different teams taking charge of the wheel alternately. Those who were taken captive might be redeemed by their successful team-mates. If one team lost more than three times it was captured. The winning team vaunted its accomplishment in the court of the other before the game proceeded.

There were several rules to this game:

1. The team which rolled the wheel the first time came only to see how the wheel was tangled and nothing was done. This was called "buying a village." This slogan has long been known to the Baganda. When a person goes to settle in a village he must first make a payment. This slogan has been adopted in many games.

2. The wheels must be tangled up only from the side where the player was supposed to stand and from nowhere else.

3. It was a forfeit if the wheel was tangled by two players of the same side. The other side did not send aimers.

4. A player might rush up and tangle the legs of one who had just tangled the wheel but had not yet moved from the court. This exempted him from having to aim at the wheel in his hand.

5. The team which rolled the wheel had the privilege of saying, "I tie my hand," to have it considered sufficient if their aimers tangled the arm holding the wheel instead of the wheel itself. If the other side shouted, "Tangle my arm," before they did, it meant that this would count as a miss and would mean a capture.

6. The side which tangled the wheel was not allowed to touch the wheel until the players of the other side had counted how many times the tangler encircled it. If they touched it the other side was exempt from the aiming.

Hockey. A game just like hockey was played.

Reed-Piercing. This game was played chiefly by goat-herders. Each player had several reeds about two feet long, divided into groups of two. One player held his piece obliquely against the ground. A player of the opposing team tried to shoot at it. If he missed they exchanged positions. If he hit it he took it up in his hand and shook it. If he had failed to smash it he put his reed down again. When a reed was smashed, he put it aside on a pile called the reed corpses. The winner was the one who succeeded in smashing all of his opponent's reeds.

Spinning Tops. [Each player spun one top, on the surface of a leaf] (37) a foot long. If one knocked the other off, the latter was

confiscated. If there were more than two players, and two tops
were knocked off at once, this was called triplex. If a player lost
all his tops he was the loser.......

Dust-Building. This was a game for small children. It was played
in a dust heap. Each had a small red grain with a dark spot on it
from an Olusiti tree. A long heap of dust was made and then the
players hid the grain in the dust. The dust was divided into several
heaps and the opposing team guessed in which of these the grain
was hidden. All the other heaps but two were scattered. If they
guessed correctly they took charge of the game. A failure counted as
a score against them.

Jack-stones. Twelve or twenty stones were used, all thrown into
the air by the first player, who tried to catch as many as he could
on the back of his hand. Then he chose a starter, and as he threw
it in the air, and before catching it, he snatched up as many as he
could of the stones on the ground. If he got no others it was not a
failure, but if the starter touched the ground he forfeited his turn.
When a player had picked up all the stones together with the starter
there were two more parts to be played. One was to pick up a little
stone which was under a big one, and then to pick up the big one.
The other was to pick up at once two stones which were twenty or
more inches apart. This constituted a score. The next score made
by the player he gave to a friend. A really excellent player was
able to give a score to everyone of the other players. This game
was a favorite with shepherds.

Colocynth Berry Game. This was played by two teams of young
men. Each team had as many as 140 berries. It was played on a
level place about twenty yards square. Each team dug a straight
line across and set down twelve berries one in each of twelve holes.
On the top of each they put a smaller berry. The opposing team
shot at the small berries of its rivals. If they used up all their
berries before knocking all the small berries off it was the turn of
the other team. The score was made by the team first knocking
off all the berries of its rival.

Sledge Game. This was for the young children. The sledge was a
plantain tree stripped of the outer bark. This was used as a toboggan
for sliding down hill.

String Game. This was played by the boys and girls together. A
piece of stick was stuck into the ground and a strong string tied
to it. The string was passed through a piece of dry calabash which
was then put into another hole in the ground, so that the string
was tightly stretched, Then the player sat down and bending the
string like a bow sang:

Sekitulege, Sekitulege, I am your sister
Sekitulege, I am your sister,
When spoken to he is dry and wriggly
Sekitulege, I am your sister.

This game was a great favorite. Sometimes the girls danced to the music. Often the older people took part too.

CHAPTER XXVIII.

MUSICAL INSTRUMENTS AND MUSIC.

These were some of the Baganda musical instruments:

[Entala. Twelve long sticks placed across two plantain stems] with small sticks to keep them apart. [In connection with this two big drums, Ntamivu and Ndoŋgo, were played. There were also two small drums, which were sounded in this manner, "When he calls, when he calls, when he calls". There was also a long instrument known as Eŋgalabi and a dancing drum Embutu. The combined sound of all these was very impressive. They are still played for the king.] (24—31)

Enteŋga. This was a sort of orchestra composed of twelve small drums, a big one, a slightly smaller one, and one known as Endoŋgo. The twelve small ones were beaten to give the song, and the other three joined in the chorus. These are still played in the palace of the king.

The songs which follow were played on enteŋga, harps, fiddle, and flutes:

Of Ensisi. Mawanda succeeded to the throne by fighting with and conquering his elder brother Kikulwe. When he had won he ordered the musicians to sing the following song:

"It was at the battle of Ensisi that the warriors were slain
It was at the battle of Ensisi that the warriors were slain."

Syphilis. Mawanda was desirous of extending his kingdom by conquest. He waged several wars against the neighboring tribes, during the course of which several women were captured. These women are said to have brought syphilis into the country. When Mawanda discovered that the hands of his warriors were becoming white from the disease, he inquired of his chiefs as to why this effect was to be noticed and was told that it was due to the cruelty of the disease. Then he ordered his musicians to play this song:

"Why is it that syphilis whitens hands?
Syphilis whitens hands because of its cruelty.
Syphilis whitens hands because of its fierceness."

"I shall buy the old." Mawanda decided to take several good looking young women to wife. Private musicians sang the following song in his honor, which pleased him so that he ordered the court musicians to play it.

"For me I shall buy an elderly one who will feed me,
For me I shall buy an elderly one who will feed me,
Because the youngsters belong to the king."

"A bald man." When Kyabagu became king he was very fond of his people and often talked to them. He was a very brave man. When he became bald the flutists played a song honoring him, which he ordered the musicians to play.

"The head of the bald man is bored (like a tree turned to powder by insects — E. B. K.)
Now he no longer seems to be a prince.
The head is bored.
Although the head is bored, he is shielding himself.
Although the head is bored, he is in the strong shield."

"Busoga Bananas Are Very Sweet." During his reign Kyabagu invaded Busoga. He had a disastrous encounter in which several warriors were killed. The others became restless and desired to return home. Kyabagu paid no heed and his musicians sang:

"If only my brother were around,
He would have heeded me.
At Busoga the spears are destroying people
If my brother only were with me
He would have allowed me to go.
At Busoga they are cutting leaves."

"Kyabagu was told." During this war the king decided that Busoga was a good country, and that he would like to annex it to his own realm. He tried to do it by pouring Baganda earth over Busoga land. Of course this scheme did not work. On his way back through Kyagwe country he angered his children and was murdered. Then the people composed this song:

"We ourselves warned Kyabagu
That a king must never in his life cross the Kiira[1]
The Kiira even though it is shallow.
No, we warned him."

---

[1] the Nile.

"Crossing the Katoŋga River." Djundju was the king who conquered Budu and annexed it. People returning from there over the Mweraŋgo River between Busiro and Mawokota counties, a very swift river which was often in flood, were often badly injured in the passage. Then they decided to come instead by the Katoŋga River, and the following song was composed and approved by the king.

> "You'd better go across Katoŋgo,
> And not Mweraŋga."

Ŋkaivu. Semakokiro staged a game. Ŋkaivu easily won it, surpassing all the other participants, and this song was composed:

> "Ŋkaivu who wears the skin of the Ŋgeye
> He will die because of racing
> Ŋkaivu will die because of racing."

"When trees were eaten." When Kamanya invaded Busoga land there was a disastrous famine, during which many people died, and all ate queer foods. When he returned to Buganda the trumpeters composed this:

> "When trees were eaten, here we come
> You may disregard anything but hunger."

Sematimba. There was a man Sewaŋkambo, of the Monkey clan, during the reign of Kamanya. He had two brothers, Sematimba and Kikwabaŋga. They were very friendly and very brave. They had a great deal of wealth in goats. Once the king declared war and these two, rejoicing, made a feast for their friends. While the food was still being prepared the general started for the front. These two followed him saying, "We shall eat when we return from the war." However they were both killed. The people composed this song in their honor:

> "Those who keep goats keep them in vain
>   See Sematimba and Kikwabaŋga
> We were many but I am all alone
>   See Sematimba and Kikwabaŋga.
>
> When I leave here I shall serve Kago
> With whom we both suffered, Kikwabaŋga
> A slow man shall find me on the floor,
> Cold, stiff, and dead, Kikwabaŋga.
>
> A mid-day caller shall find me under the dry grass
> Speechless and motionless under the dry grass.
> If you hate me you shall hate the child,
> See Sematimba, Kikwabaŋga."

"A little male animal will wipe out the people." One day Se-waŋkambo Sekibobo was made a general to attack the Busoga tribe. He killed several people and they said, "This is a small animal from Buganda to wipe us out." When the Baganda musicians heard this, they composed the following song:

"The little animal from Buganda
Shall wipe out the people
The little male animal from Buganda
Shall wipe out all the warriors."

"Destruction." It is a well known fact that Kamanya was a hero and that he waged two or three wars a month. Then the people sang "Kamanya's things are eaten with shields."[1] This pleased the king and he ordered his musicians to play it.

"I walk like a Muhima." When Suna became king there was a famine. The Bahima people worked very hard to supply their masters with milk. Those who were suffering from hunger saw these people with milk and thought they were not suffering so they composed this song:

"I shall walk like a Muhima
And be saved from hunger at Mulago
I shall walk like a Muhima
And be saved from this injurious situation."

"If I had wings." During the reign of Suna, many people became very much concerned about death. They therefore composed this song:

"If I had wings I should have flown,
Because our ancestors all are gone.
If I had wings I should have flown."

"All chiefs must go." King Suna was very fond of hunting. He made his uncle Sebanakita Kagenda head of the hunt. He loved him very much and made many of the strongest men go to the village of his uncle. Because of the honor in which the king held him the following song to him was composed:

"A husky woman, she drinks like a man.
When you see her you take her for a man
When she returns home she asks for the food."

"They have appointed Mukwenda." King Suna appointed Mu-kwenda Seŋkatuka to fight at Gambalagala. The expedition lasted for several months and the warriors were severely attacked by dis-

---

[1] This has referance to the oath of allegiance in war, in which food is taken with shield on arm — EBK.

eases. When the general went through the line he never paid any
attention to those who were sitting down because they were sick.
So the trumpeters composed this song:

> "Whom have they appointed?
> They have appointed Mukwenda.
> Mukwenda who knows not suffering.
> Whom have they appointed? Mukwenda.
> Who is Mukwenda? Mukwenda who knows not suffering."

Ntwere. In the days of Suna there was a man named Ntwere. He
was a musician who played the trumpet. One day the group went
to the palace to play for the king. In the interval while they were
resting Ntwere went around smoking his pipe. Just then the king
arrived to listen to the music. Ntwere stuck his pipe into the barkcloth bag under his skin dress. The music started and as Ntwere
played he jumped and danced about. The fire caught the bag and
burned through the skin dress. When the king observed the smoke
he said, "Ntwere, why do you smoke like that?" When he explained
the king ordered him to undress at once. It was then discovered that
his side was already badly burned. The king, and the court laughed,
and the following song was played:

> "Ntwere, you are twisting your back
> Your rough skin will catch fire."

"I am going to Buganda to drink a little sweet beer." Suna
invaded Busoga and all the Basoga went to an island Kitente. Suna
besieged this island and won the battle. When the Basoga retreated
the first man of their army went out to meet the king. He had four
vessels with him. When the king asked him why, he said that he was
going to Buganda to drink some sweet beer. The king was pleased
and ordered the following song played:

> "I am going to Buganda to drink sweet beer
> I am going to Buganda to drink.
> Famine destroyed Kitente
> I am going to Buganda to drink sweet beer."

"Rudeness makes them climb trees."[1] When Suna became king
he asked why Djundju and Semakokiro, sons of the same mother,
had fought, and then he himself gave the answer,

> "It was their rudeness, that is why they fought."

"War declared at Naligaba." Suna while he was at Nabulagala
decided to invade Busagala. He ordered his drummer Kaula to
sound the royal drum Mudjaguzo on Lubya hill. When Suna return-

---

[1] As is the case with upper-class children. E. B. K.

ed from the war the trumpters composed this song to remind him that if there was anyone in the land unmindful of his decrees, he must be subdued.

> "He dispatched the army from Lubya
> The old man dispatched it from Lubya
> Let Mudjaguzo sound.
> He dispatched it from Lubya."

"It was at Wadjala." One day Suna went to Lusaka and had a very merry feast. The king himself composed this song:

> "Such a great merriment was at Wadjala
> Behold a great merriment at Wadjala
> Being the least one I missed that great merriment.
> Such a great merriment was at Wadjala."

"A hole in the checker-game gave birth to a royal thing." When Suna died his son Mukabya succeeded him. He was a very good and handsome young man whom all the people admired greatly. They composed a song:

> "Out of a cruel thing (Suna) came forth a precious thing.
> He who does not know the precious thing, it is Mutesa.
> Out of a cruel thing came forth a precious thing.
> Banda the city of Mutesa
> Which we inhabit — receiving salt and meat from him.
> Out of a cruel thing came forth a precious thing.
> He who does not know the precious thing, it is Mutesa.
> Out of a cruel thing came forth a precious thing.
> Those who build the palace really do build
> Those who build the city really do build.
> Those who build another palace really do build.
>   Oh,
> Out of a cruel thing came forth a precious thing."

"Those who despised him." When Walugembe ascended the throne, he had a very youthful appearance. Several of his brothers were older and stronger. This caused disrespect on the part of several of the chiefs, who finally rebelled against him. The chiefs conspired to steal from the palace those of the princes whom they were backing for the kingship. Very intelligently and calmly Mukabya took counsel with his prime minister Kaira and the other chiefs who were remaining loyal, and quelled the rebellion. The conspirators were all seized and put do death. The following song was thus inspired:

10

> "Those who despised his youthfulness
> Today are paying the penalty
> Those who despised his youthfulness
> Today are giving gifts."

"I warned you." When Mutesa established Banda city, he exhibited his ferocious disposition. Several people were arrested and put to death. Great terror was created and afterwards the people would say of a man who had been killed, "I warned so-and-so not to go out on the street but he would pay no heed." From this the king ordered a song sung:

> "I warned you but you paid no heed
> Now the lion has devoured you."

Nandjobe. When Mutesa assassinated Mukwenda Nduga he confiscated his wives. Among them was a woman who was the mother of Diba Omulwaza. When she came to the palace she gave birth to a princess, who was named Nandjobe. When the musicians saw that she resembled Diba, they sang:

> "Nandjobe the child resembles Diba
> See, Nandjobe resembles Diba."

"Those who pray with water." Mutesa founded a city at Nakawa. There he began his profession of the Mohammedan religion. He passed a decree enjoining a fast upon all the people. This song was sung:

> "The water-fasters do not eat dinners.
> They are depending upon a Mohammedan feast."

Nakyadjwe. This was a boat belonging to Sabaganzi, which was seized by the Bavuma, only to be blown back by the wind at night. The Baganda musicians saw it and sang:

> "Nakyadjwe objected,
> I am a Muganda citizen,
> I refuse to go with Bagwe,
> The good council of Mutesa
> Increases his subjects."

"He means what he decrees." Mutesa once passed a decree against a black goat, potatoes, and beans. The musicians sang:

> He means what he decrees
> Kabaka Mukabya
> He means what he decrees."

"Who sold him the beer ?" When Mwaŋga II became king he was
very fond of fat meat. When this was not donated to him he seized
it by force. The musicians sang:

> "Who sold him beer ?
> Today we are giving him goods
> Today we are giving him gifts."

This was a very popular song especially among the pages. When it
was played these manly gentlemen walked in a dignified fashion.
When they met anyone who did not belong to their division they
chased him off the street like a small animal.

"He who has never seen a gun." Mwaŋga was very fond of
soldiery. He organized several battalions of strong young men, and
many, in order to be assigned to these, brought presents of guns, as
only those who had guns were allowed to be appointed. Then the
musicians composed this song:

> "He who has never seen a gun, let him go to Meŋgo.
> Those who hang around at Meŋgo, every page must fight."

Bagalayaze. This was sung as a memorial to that queen mother.

> "Bagalayaze, feed upon your cows
>   And have vegetables to congratulate yourself.
> Bagalayaze, prepare a big beef feast
>   And feed the pages."

"I do not need clothes." One of the reasons for the composition
of this song was the praise of Mwaŋga. Another was to ask him for
goods. The Abapere division of the pages was allowed to do just
as it liked while this song was sung.

> "I do not need to buy clothes
>   Mwaŋga will provide for me.
> I do not need to buy clothes
>   The king will provide for me."

"Omunyoro who kicks." The growing European population helped Mwaŋga to fight against his brother Kalema. At first there was a
strong friendship between the king and the Europeans, but he grew
distrustful of them. The ladies in the palace of Mutesa's father heard
this and sang:

> "Let Suna be told where he is at Wamala
> Of this Omunyoro who kicks
>   Whom are you kicking against ?
> And also Kamanya at Kasadja
>   Let him be told.

10*

> Kabaka Mwaŋga spends his days at Kampala
> He will suffer the consequences
> Woe to him the son of Mutesa
> You, the Omunyoro who kicks,
>   Whom are you kicking against ?"

This song was meant as an insult but the king was very fond of it.
Boating. Mwaŋga was very fond of the lake. This boating song
was composed for him:

> "Boating Boating
>   And no one to row them
> I shall inquire at Batanda
>   Is the king at Busabala.
>
> A husky man is like a rooster
>   When the king is away he fasts
> I shall inquire from Batanda
>   If the king is at Busabala."

Kisiŋgiri. This is a country near Kisumu. Here the merchants
used to import salt in the days of Mwaŋga. The people came to like
salt very much. It was called after the name of this country.

> "Kisiŋgiri is one sweet vegetable
> When you mix it in the vegetable
> It tastes very sweet.
> Kisiŋgiri our head.
> When you taste it once and for all,
> Kisiŋgiri our, sweet vegetable."

"I am going down to the harbor." In the old days it was very
hard to persuade a fisherman to visit Buganda. When he was invited
to do so, he would say, "With whom shall I leave my nets ?" To
these fisherman their nets were the most important things in the
world. When the trumpeters heard of this they composed the
following song:

> "I am going down to throw my nets,
> The nets that keep me busy.
> I am going down to throw my nets,
> The nets that keep me from visiting Buganda."

There were certain sorts of calabashes which the trumpeters used.
These were highly thought of among the royal instruments. There
were several songs which were favorites with the king which were
particularly adapted to this instrument. Some of these have been
printed.

"I have found the large birds feeding." This song was played
whenever the king became very angry, as when he ordered a large-
scale human killing.

"I have found the large birds feeding.
I have found the large birds picking.
I have found them feeding and picking."

"They will remember his going." When the king indulged in day
dreams and thought about death, he would order this song played:

"They will remember the old man
Those who eat with him will remember after death
Will remember his Majesty after death.
Those who eat with him will remember his Majesty after his
  death."

There were in all about a dozen or two flutes. There were two
dancing drums and an eŋgalabi associated with them. Played
together they produced a fine harmony. There were four holes on
the flute, with one other at the mouth. (Roscoe says flutes had six
holes.)

[Greetings.....] (42) When the guest had been greeted he was
given a smoke and a small basket of roasted coffee grains. Then the
women left and went to prepare food for the guests. The guests
were fed upon a goat, or if this was not possible, upon sweet vegetables. If they were not given a smoke they became very dissatis-
fied. From this customary use of tobacco came the proverb, "Eat
first after a smoke."

CHAPTER XXIX.

FISHING

...[Ropes for fishing were made out of a special grass] called
obuyandja. This was dried and twisted all in one day. The twisting
had at least to be started on the day of the drying. The ropes were
called kyuŋgo or kyamba. [Mats 100 feet by 8 were made of water
grass or bulrushes,] and three ropes were plaited of a certain water
grass. On top of the plaited ropes twelve nets were put. These were
known as nindwe. On the one side were four small nets known as
bagota and on the other basenyi. [The mat was put on top of this
with several stones to hold the whole under the water in the lake.]
(392)

A rope attached to the net was carried about 400 feet out and
there fastened with a large stone. The place was circled in this

manner. A small branched stick attached to a canoe held the rope, so that the presence of fish might be indicated. Then the net was placed under the water and fastened. The group on shore then pulled, and all stamped their feet until the fish entered the net. There was a taboo about the small fish known as ŋkedje that the first two which were fished out might not be eaten by a man who had known his wife the night before. If this taboo were broken it was believed that none of these would ever be fished again.

If the head fisherman found a decrease in the number of fish caught he suspected someone of having done something wrong. He would therefore call the group together and endeavor to find the guilty man. If he confessed, the captain drew several strips of leaves and held them in his hand, praying, "O Mukasa! We will not offend again. The guilty person has been found. Give!"

Having offered the prayer he dropped the leaves and they all took the net and cast it in the lake.

[When enough fish had been caught the captain knew his wife.] (393) The third time he ordered all the fishermen to know their wives, as the net had been purified and there was nothing to fear.

In the distribution of fish all divided equally. If anyone complained it was believed that Mukasa would allow no more fish to be caught. The rope maker was also prohibited from knowing his wife until after the first two rounds of the fishing.

There were a group of fishermen called Abasambazi who had no taboos about their fishing. They had herbs known as muluku which they mixed in the waters they were using for fishing grounds. The fish died of the poisonous water and then were merely picked off the top. This kind of fishing was mostly carried out in small rivers and pools.

The fishermen who specialized in bream (engege) had enormous nets, which they cast very expertly. First they measured the distance from the shore and used trees in the village for alignment. A three-branched stick to which a rope was attached and a stone to hold down the net were part of the equipment. . . . .

There was a group which specialized in the capture of lungfish. These had large dragnets known as kabugu. They dug several holes in a meadow-like place near the sea and in these they put the stalks of a water-lily upon which the fish was supposed to feed. Under the holes they secured the dragnets. The fish saw the grass, came up to eat it, and so was caught.

[Some small fish were caught with worms and insects. . . .] (397)

When a canoe was launched for the first time the owner was entitled to the fish in any dragnet he came upon. This was part of the regular canoe building ceremony, (the beginning of it is here the same as in Roscoe, page 388) and after this he was allowed to have intercourse with his wife.

CHAPTER XXX

CANOE BUILDING.

Generally the oak was used for the principal part of the canoe. Those for the king were made ceremoniously. Gabuŋga, the admiral, or some other chief was appointed to supervise construction. There were special tools used for this purpose. Naŋkuŋgo and Bulya-munyama were the two steel axes. These were in the custody of Mayandja of the Bird clan when they were not in use.

When they came to the forest to fell the oak with the axe Naŋkuŋgo, the man who did the cutting addressed the tree as follows: "It is not I who order myself to cut you, but Naŋkuŋgo." In this manner the bad luck was offset and death averted.

In order to avoid splitting of the tree, the lateral roots were cut and the tree dug up. Then the length and diameters were measured, and cut. The boat when done was from ten to fifteen feet long on the inside.

The branches and roots of the tree were cut off, and the sides trimmed. Then the inside of the trunk was hollowed, the top being taken off, to safeguard it against rotting. Then the front and rear were pointed somewhat and the bottom flattened. Then the whole was carried on rolling logs to the dockyard. These logs had to be of soft wood so that the main trunk would not be scratched or injured by them.

For the sides of the canoes certain trees were preferred. These were emiyovu and ŋkoba. These were hard enough to withstand any sort of weather and obviate any danger of leakage.

The king's boats and some of the others were constructed by experts who were trained in the trade from childhood. Different parts required different experts, who knew what to do and what not to do. Special tools belonged to each of these.

One of these was Omutusa. He had big and small knives and axes. Some of these were:

Ndjeyo	to cut wood for making fires.
Nsuma	to cut the edges and smooth the inside and bottom of the boat
Kikumbi	a very wide and sharp axe for finishing
Kayeyo katono	the smallest of them all. Used to smooth the seats, and make the holes for the fastenings.

Kayozo   a little axe with two teeth, used to carve and
                          decorate the edges and other parts of the boat.

All the parts of the boat were separately done as perfectly as
possible. Then the whole was put together. There was a great deal
of skill necessary, for all the parts had to be carefully measured so
that they would fit together. Cinders were generally used to mark
the spots where the connections were going to be. The opposite
boards had to be cut and finished in such fashion that their weights
would be the same, lest the whole overbalance to one side. The main
trunk was held down with heavy stones, the side boards with heavy
pegs nailed against them, to avoid warping.

To fit the parts together, holes were drilled with hot spikes, and
through these pegs or skin thread were drawn. All the holes had to
be tightly filled. There had to be especial care taken about the front
part of the boat because of the danger of waves.

When the body of the boat was finished, the anchor was fastened
in front and the seats inserted. They were tightly fastened and
comfortable. They were generally made of emifulumbwa trees.

Most boats had four side boards, and as many seats as they could
be made to hold. They were also supplementary boards, such as the
one joining the tip of the prow to the body of the boat.

Horns of an animal were set upon the prow as a symbol of
strength. They were supposed to give the impression of a living
animal. The upper part of the boat was painted with clay mixed with
corn beer. For decoration the owner might decide to add bird
feathers, a goat skin, or other decorations. These might be depictions
of a living animal, particularly of the symbol of the clan.

The oars were all of the same length and breath, except those of
the pilot.

When the boat was ready, it was launched and tested amid shouts
and applause, the wives being the main spectators.

At the start of the work, before the felling of the tree, a virgin boy
was required to cut a piece of the tree and then to burn it. He had
then to keep to himself till the work was done. This brought luck
both to the builders and the boat.

CHAPTER XXXI.
THE NAVY.

The following is an account of the navy. [Gabuŋga was the
admiral. All chiefs whose boundaries touched the lake were bound
to own canoes.] (382—384) This included Kyagwe, Bulondoganyi,
Nakakweya, Bugugu, Budu, Budjadju, and Dumu.

Busiro County.

Canoe	Captain	Place kept	Clan
Kiwanuka	Gabuŋga	Nakubidje	Mamba
Namutebi		Naŋgombe	
Ntamunyaŋgu	Kalyaŋgo	Buvi	Ŋgo
Direndjogera	Mugula	Buira, Ntebe	Mamba
Kigonya	Magera	Gatinda, Busi	,,
Kairigi	Kabadja	Kiboga	,,
Namutebi II	Wasanyi	Kiguŋgu	,,
Nakibuka	Mukalazi	Kagulube, Ziba	,,
Waswa	Kiyaga	Balemutwe	,,
Nakasiga	Mulumba	Lwandjaba	,,
Nakibuka II	Kalega	Kyasira	,,
Namutebi III	Miro	Nakalembe, Ziŋga	,,
Magezigom	Galabuzi	Ŋkuba	,,
Demberere	Kasunsa	Ntabwo	,,
Nagaŋga	Ganantawa	Mbiru	Nyonyi
Nanyoŋga	Mugaŋga	Kagolomolo	,,
Namuyandja	Muyandja	Mukaka (Bugeme)	,,
Kinyenyentuntu	Mwota	Kagave Nalugala	Nvuma
Nakerebwe	Nawalyaŋga	Sazi	Fumbe
Namunyi	Fulu	Kasenyi	,,
Kanyenyeŋkule	Nawambwa	Bugabo	Mbogo
Wagumbulizi	Sebugwawo	Kogero	Musu
Waswa II	Nakiyendje	Bukasa	Ndiga
Namugambe	Mugambe	Ziŋga	Mpewo
Nakasi	Serugomera	Kyulwe	Mamba
Mubisi	Malagala	Kibale	Ŋkima
Naloŋgo	This was kept in the Ekikasa division of the king's pages at Bwegeyero.		

Kyadondo County.

Waswa	Kikambi	Busabala	Lugave

This was the royal yacht used by the kings for cruising.

Kairigi	Nampyaŋgu	Kadzi	Fumbe
Kudjemera	Wakikuŋga	Mutuŋgo	Ndiga

When this captain became the king's favorite, he took charge of all the fleet.

Nakibuka	Nsimbi	Kadzi	Ndjovu
Nakitanda	Kakembo	Ziranumbu	,,

Kyagwe County.

Canoe	Captain	Place Kept	Clan
Naloŋgo	Kikwata (Rear Admiral)	Batale	Ŋkedje
Nalubuŋga		Gamba	
Mbaliga	Seryenvu	Kisinsi	Fumbe
(This was Mwaŋga's favorite after Waswa.)			
Kawase	Lugumba	Bukodi	Nvuma
Namagulu	Myamba	Lukolo	Lugave
Waswa	Kiwagu	Gombe	Ndiga
Nakyedjwe	Namaba	Kodja	Mamba
Kisima	Namfu-mbambi	Kyesimira	Nsenene
Nakasa	Nakaima	Kirudu	Musu
Nakate	Musoke	Kisinsi	Ndjovu
Lugemaŋkofu	Naŋkanyaga	Kisenyi	Nyonyi
Kiriŋgiride	Sebuira	Sugu	Mpewo
Batambuzakyaŋga	Namugwaŋga	Gwowo	Lugave
Direndjogera	Ntambi	Nalumuli	Ndjovu
Nalyadzi	Mufumula	Nyim	Nvuma
Watuleŋgunda	Mawande		Mamba
Namukasa	Kamyoka Kiriŋgo	Senyi	Mpindi
Mulyambuzi	Kamyoka Nambeta	Naluŋgu	
Nakabugo I	Mukotanyi	Nadjundju	Ŋkima
Kintulugumen-yandja	Ŋkakya	Gamba	Mpewo
Nakitaṅda I	Kirisa	Kituntu	Ndjaza
Namukasa	Mulinda	Busagazi	Mamba
Nakitanda II	Ndjuki	Kigombe	Mamba
Namunyomba	Muyomba	Kabugoga	Nyonyi
Nakabugo II	Nalumu	Nsoŋga	Ŋkima

The following canoes were located at Kome, Damba, Lwadje, and Bwema islands and were all under the supervision of Kikwata:

Tadjemerwa	Nyendje	Kibaŋga, Kome	Mamba
Mukwanogwe-nyandja	Sekoba	Saŋga	Ndiga
Kawomera	Semagoŋge	Kome	Butiko
Kiriwagulu	Kimuli	Lwazimiruli	Musu
Kirimuŋgo	Sekolo	Lwadje	Nvuma

Canoe	Captain	Place kept	Clan
Ŋkenenyi	Kibomba	Damba	Mamba
Ŋkwanzi	Nabefunye	Kitaka	
Musoke	Lusadjalubi	Mawembe	Ŋoŋge
Nalugonda	Lukonda	Bwema	
Nakakweya	Kiwana	Bukweya harbor at Bulondoganyi	Nvuma

Budu County.

Nakauŋgu	Kasumba	Kaziru, Budjadju	Kasimba

Sese Islands.

Canoe	Captain	Place kept	Clan
Nanemba	Kaganda	Bugoŋga, Bukasa	Ŋoŋge
Kinyenyentuntu	Mwonda	Mabaŋga Bugeme	
Kiriwagulu	Sendege	Namirembe Bugeme	
Nalubale	Sekamalira	Bukasa	
Kyamubinire	Serukundi	Ŋkandaga Mukene	
Kawomera	Semuwabula	Lugu	Ŋkima
Somboza	Musala	Soko	,,
Namulindi	Maso	Semunya, Fuŋve	,,
Mukulwalimanyika	Semugala	Lukalu, Bugala	,,
Kasolo	Serumaga	Mugera	Nvubu
Muira	Gere	Nsa	Lugave
Musoke II	Kiboŋgo	Makoko	Nyonyi
Kiyola	Semukade	Bulega	Mamba
Kikutira	Bugimbi	Dadje	,,
Naŋfuka	Semuindi	Kisoko	,,
Nalyambe	Sewaya	Lukindu	,,
Ŋkoŋge	Sekalala	Nabisasiro	,,
Nadjoge	Businde	Kasekulo	,,
Nansoŋga	Sekibo	Kibaŋga	,,
Namutebi	Sekalere	Namirembe	,,
Nakiryowa	Sekiryowa	Nsazi	,,
Walyolumbe	Serinya	Nakibuka	,,
Namulima	Semugogo	Kawafu, at Bubeke	,,
Direndjogera	Musala	Ntuba	,,
Nantai	Katonya	Musisi	,,
Wanabira	Luvule	Serinya at Lulamba	,,
Mbogewagula	Namalubi	Kalo, at Djana	,,
Kawomera	Namuyimba	Mukaka	Ŋoŋge
Namugaŋga	Kawali	Kondjero Bufimira	,,

Canoe	Captain	Place kept	Clan
Namuganga II	Katanda	Nalwenaga, Bugaba	Donge
Sikamukazi	Gugu	Musove	Bugeme
Nambwa	Lubobi	Namwambula Buvu	Fumbe

There were in all 104 canoes, under the jurisdiction of Gabunga, who was one of the most respected men in the kingdom although he was not a feudal chief. The navy when launched, with all the additional vessels of the chiefs and the fishermen, numbered 10,000 vessels.

The Islands.

Bugala was the largest of the islands, in size and population... Some outstanding nobles such as Semugala of the Dkima clan, Musala and Semuwabula of the same clan, Serumaga of the Nvumu clan, Gere of the Lugave clan, Semukade, Bugimbi, Semuindi, Sekalala, and Businda all of the Mamba clan, were all located here.

Bukasa island boasted Kaganda as chief landlord, who belonged to the Donge clan. Sekalere of the Mamba clan, and Muwonda and Sendege of the Nvumu clan, were also of this island.

The chief landlords of the other islands:

Buuvu	Lubobi of the Fumbe clan
Funve	Maso of the Dkima clan
Bugaba	Katanda of the Donge clan
Bafumira	Namuyimba I ,,
Buyovu	Namuyimba ,,
Bundjazi	Kamenyangabo ,,
Katabo	Kaunya of the Mamba clan
Lulamba .	Musala II of the Dkima clan
Kome	Nyendje of the Mamba clan

The people of Kome island were known as Bakome, those of Damba as Balamba, and the chief of the latter was Kibomba, Mamba clan. The feudal chief of Bulago island, Semugombe, also belonged to the Mamba clan. The people of these three islands were not native Basese, but Basese Bagwe, or Bavuma Abakandja, since they knocked out one of the teeth of the lower jaw.

Damba	Sekibango, Lugave clan
Tavu	Senambwa, Mbogo clan
Sowe	Katabo, Mamba clan

These islands are all rich and fertile. They raise good bananas, sweet potatoes, yams and coffee. These sixteen islands fed all of Buganda during the hard times during the war of 1890.

Kibibi	Kawuŋga,	Ŋkima clan
Buigi	Semirembe	,,
Butulume	Ntulume	Mutima clan
Kirugu	Semuwanda	,,
Bugembe	Gugu	Bugume clan
Ziru	Namuyimba	,,
Bubeke	Semugogo,	Mamba clan
	Musala	,,
	Katonya	,,
Kuye	Semukwiri	,,
Djana	Namalubi	,,
Buyaŋga	Sekisero	,,
Serinya	Luvule	,,
Kibibi II	Semumira	,,
Nsazi	Serinya	,,
Kimi	Sekitula	,,

These islands are also very nice. The people produce yams, potatoes and the like.

Ludjabwa	Semukade of the Nyonyi clan. This island is rich because of its abundance of fish.
Saŋga	Sabaganzi, the king's uncle
Mukusu	Lusadjalubi, chief of the Mamba clan
Buliŋguge	Kakembo, chief of the Ndjovu clan
Namalusu } Kiruba }	These both belong to Kago

These six islands were used chiefly for fishing.

Bunyama	Mugiŋga of Bugeme, known for its parrots.
Banda	Sekirika, Mamba clan. On this island the special grass used in the making of fishing canoes was grown, in addition to the more usual things.
Lwaŋga	Kabogo of the Ŋkima clan. Only potatoes were grown.

The remaining islands are barren because they are rocky.
Mwana is noted for its many brindled gnu.

Mbugwe	Linzira	Kabale	Mweza	Kakide	Semanya
Liŋga	Manene	Namabega	Kataŋga	Limaiba	Luke

Kansove I	Kansove II	Matinda	Lunva	Kizima	Mawanyi
Mbive I	Mbive II	Lugazi II	Luserera	Lwaŋga	Nambu
Mawu	Nabweŋku-lume	Buyuŋge	Kampiri	Nabu-soŋke	
Mawungwe	Sekaziŋga	Lyabulume	Lugazi	Ŋkovu	Kamu-kula
Nziribandje	Kiserwa	Kawaga	Kabula-taka		Ŋkose
Lwansendwe	Ŋgabo I	Ŋgabo II	Masirye	Ŋkese	Mirigi
Namiryaŋgo	Kasadja	Kantote	Nsirwe	Landa	Mbirubu-ziba
Kalambide	Nfo	Kolima	Kakunyu	Ŋkuzi	Sali Lwa-bana

On a few of these rubber can be grown. On the other hand the people of Sese were not farmers and their women did not utilize the soil, which was fairly fertile. They gossiped too much of the time.

Buvuma was the largest of its group. The others were:

Buyaga	Buziri	Liŋgira	Mpata
Lufu	Meru	Ziri	Lukalu
Nyenda	Mpaga	Kiwa	Ziri
Nambulambwalo	Kireŋge	Bwema	Watwe
Kibibi	Malidja	Makali	
Lwadje	Ziriwandjebi	Sagamba	
Luwero	Kyakisima	Bwema	
Lwamafuta	Kaziŋga	Igwe	

These thirty and the Sese eighty-nine make 119 islands. These are in Lake Nalubale, the Victoria Nyanza.. They formed Kweba and Mbubi counties.

Although the Abavuma were dependent on others for the rest of their food supply, they got lots of fish. They were very brave, and adept at seafaring. [They maintained a large fleet and were very highly respected for their abilities in warfare.] (254)

. (Roscoe says that the Bavuma do not consider themselves to be under the jurisdiction of the Baganda, and often fight with them.)

CHAPTER XXXII.

POTTERY.

The potter had first to pulverize gravel and very hard rocks into a powder of the consistency of sand. [The clay was stored in a pit] and covered with the wet decayed pith of a plantain stem, which

kept it from drying. [The clay and gravel were mixed] (399) on a
cowhide [to the proper working consistency and the result rolled
into long strips for coiling.] They were made on a mat of dried
leaves, and left there till the next day.

[The bottom was shaped like a flat saucer and then the rolled
strips coiled on to this to the desired height. This was the first or
rough stage. It was followed by the process of polishing with a piece]
the size of the hand [broken from a dry gourd] dipped in water
and used to smooth the inside. [After this a roll was applied at the
top to make the rim.] Designs were then carved on the pot near the
rim. The pot was then left in the house for two days, when it was
turned over and the bottom finished. [For ten days more the drying
continued after which it was set in the sun a few times and then
fired]...... Before the pots were finished they were known as
Myoli.

The art of pottery seems to have been known during Kintu's
reign. It was thought that Sekayala was the first potter. He did his
job so well that Kintu recognized his ability and renamed him
Sedagala. During the preparation of the clay he sang the following
song:

> Sedagala makes pots, he makes pots that get dry.
> Sedagala makes pots, he makes pots that get dry.

This was a favorite of the potters. He became known and was
respected until Kamanya's reign. When Kamanya became king
he captured a Munyoro, Kawonawo Banda. With him were captured
his men and others to the number of about 3000 souls. The king
asked him what his occupation had been, and Banda said, "My
trade is that of the potter. I know how to make pots and jars."
The king then permitted him to go on with his old trade. This he
did so admirably that he was soon recognized as the king's potter.
He was given the village Nakigalala for his own permanent use.
Although Sedagala remained at the head of the pottery department
his work was somewhat slighted and his prestige decreased.

Clay was not dug when the moon had just appeared. Any dug
then had "amasumi" and pots from it would not last long. Pots
which were fired at this time would go to pieces in the kiln. (R. says
there was no firing after the full of the moon.)

Potters were among those exempt from the risk of sudden
execution. They were highly respected, and so were their pots.
Anyone who broke one before the maker was "a fool for breaking
the people's nurse." This was because the pots were looked upon as
the source of food, which sustains life.

In the old days in the course of a war the invaders might seize all the people and their property, but the pots were always left where they were. They were used for cooking by marauders but they were never broken or stolen. If the owners regained their liberty they could come back and find them unmolested.

CHAPTER XXXIII.

METAL WORKING.

The pit for smelting was lined with seaweed pith. (R. says clay.) (379)

The coal used was from the emizanvuma, nongo, mitampindi, and misese trees..........

Worn out tools of all sorts were taken to the smith to be remade into something else. The craft has been dying of late and there are very few men able to work metal as they could in the old days. The knowledge of smelting was acquired originally from the Banyoro and Banabudu.

During Nakibinge's reign the blacksmiths were the king's favorites because they made deadly arrows and spears which helped to conquer the enemies with which he was surrounded on all sides. The story is told how at one time the fighting was going on and finally all the iron for weapons was exhausted. The queen then supplied the army with reeds so the fighting could go on.

It was Mawanda who received Kongonge of the Banyoro, whose occupation was that of smelter. He gave him an estate in Kyagwe county and employed him as smelter, many of the rocks near the coast being found to be ore-bearing.

When Djundju annexed Budu territory he imported and employed several qualified smiths.

Walukaga of the Kisimba clan was the head of all the blacksmiths. His estate was at Kiruga in Butambala county. Each county also had its own head smith.

Name	Clan	County
Wamala,	Ŋgeye	Siŋgo
Bamuŋgiriza,	Mamba	Kyagwe
Naŋkyama,	Lugave	Bulemezi
Serugoti,	Mamba	Busiro
Kaiwa,	Kobe	Mawokota
Mutagubya,	Nte	Budu

The blacksmiths also were exempt from arbitrary arrest and killing, and carried hammers, as emblems of their calling, for protection.

The smith's trade was one of the less profitable ones, though it is said that they became wealthier by sticking to their anvils. The trouble lay in the low rates gotten for the conversion of metal tools into others. The manufacture of some objects paid rather well, fifty cowry shells being the price of a hoe, axe, spear, or large knife, but a small knife or razor would bring only one or two cowry shells. Sometimes the customer paid in beer, plantain food, etc., instead of cash.

The Baganda blacksmiths did not have copper but were able to use it. They made headgear of various sorts. One design was called hornbill because when two of them met it was like a hornbill. During the reign of Djundju there was a great deal of trade in copper with the Banakalagwe.

CHAPTER XXXIV.

TABOOS.

There were very rigorous taboos in Buganda. For practically every undertaking there were precautionary taboos which had to be observed. Most of these had to do with women.

Women were looked down upon and in many respects completely segregated. They were not permitted to touch things that the men were doing. When a diviner was foretelling the future for a man he would tell him not to have any relations with his wife for a certain period. Failure to observe this was the same as breaking his vow before the diviner, and this was thought to be the cause should his undertaking prove unsuccessful. If a man could not bear the restrictions imposed on him by the diviner, he would come and ask to have them suspended for a day or so. If this was granted he might then have relations with his wife.

[A man setting out on a journey would return if he met a woman first.] (17) If he had gone a long way, and did not turn back, he would expect some bad luck in connection with the trip.

This segregation of the female sex may have been due to the fact that according to the creation story it was Nambi Nantutululu, the wife of Kintu, who on account of her disobedience brought Mr. Death with her and destroyed several of Kintu's children. It was thought that this had a great deal to do with the suffering of women.

All the observances with regard to women were strictly carried out.

11

CHAPTER XXXV

CHARACTERISTICS OF VARIOUS GROUPS.

Kyadondo County.

The people in this county were perhaps the most intelligent in the kingdom. This was one of the chief reasons why [the kings established their capitals here.] Another was the presence of numerous lakes. The county was, however, not a wealthy one, and though [the county chief was the highest ranking one in the country] (248) he was often surpassed by others in wealth, because he could not raise as much in taxes.

The river Mayandja rises in Kyadondo.

Plantains and bananas, the chief Buganda foods, were not very plentiful in Kyadondo, so that they depended rather upon sweet potatoes and other products. .

The king's army of execution was located here. They helped to carry out all his orders. Some of the regiments were:

Divisions	Leaders:	
Kiwenda	Seŋkole	Lugave clan
Kisigula	Mpiŋga	Lugave clan
Kimbale	Sebata	Ŋgeye clan

Siŋgo County.

This was the largest and most populated (R. says it was sparsely populated) of all the counties. Until 1892 [it included also Buwekula which then became a separate county.] (249) The people were intelligent and home loving. When they had business away from home, even at the capital, they would transact it and hurry home. Men from Siŋgo rarely visited the capital.

The large population made for a plentitude of taxable items. This was particularly true of the trade in salt and hoes, and cattle raising. Kitesa and Kyanamugera had the best pasture land.

There are three rivers which were much used for fishing — Nabakazi, Bimbye, and Kitumbi. Namatamba hill and Kyato at Kiterega were very beautiful spots in the county. Famine was never known here.

[Kyagwe County.] (251)

This county was divided into three sections. Those of the first of these were like the Basoga; but the Bagola and Bakundja of the coast resembled the Abavuma in language and manners. These people were noted for their skill in the manufacture of musical instruments, and they originated the two royal drums known as Entamiv and Entenga. They were brave warriors, skilled in the use of the spear. For a long time the people recognised neither the county chief, nor the king himself.

The second or Bukoba part was inhabited by intelligent people who resembled the people of Bulemezi in language and skill. Cattle, goats, sheep and ivory were the chief wealth of the people and the soil was fertile and yielded a good banana crop. The chief was also enriched by an annual tax paid him by some of [the Basoga over whom he had control.] (250)

The third part was known as Mabira or forest. The forest was infested by millions of tiny bloodsucking insects. These injured the veins so that the foresters were called dwarfs because of their small size. Strange stories were told about them such as that they do not marry and cannot have children. (cf. p. 123)

At Kasai and Mpoma in Kyagwe there was a plentiful coffee crop, which was said to be the sweetest for chewing in the country.

There are three large rivers, Lwadjali, separating Kyadondo and Bulemezi counties, Sezibwa, and Musanya. These three rivers meet and flow in one vast body into the Nile.

Bulemezi County.

The people of this county were noted for their linguistic ability. In the old days, the peasants would visit the chiefs and use all sorts of humorous phrases, thus pleasing them greatly. They made feasts for them and gave them gifts. In some cases small children were versed in joke-telling and joined in the conversation.

The county was however not wealthy and most of the people were poor. Most of the barkcloth was imported from Busiro and Mawokota. This shortage was due to the fact that the barkcloth tree dried and died soon here. There were two sections, Busubika and Matembe, which were prosperous in cattle raising, but for the most part the cattle perished by some introduced disease.

Lugogo is the only big river. It flows right through the county. The two capitals, at Buzinde and Kasaga, founded by Kintu, were the only ones ever established here.

Busiro County.

This county was popular as a place for the kings to establish their capitals. [It was also the place for the royal burials.] (252) The

11*

people were noted for their knowledge of languages, particularly
Luganda. This was due to the presence of a great number of princesses whose speech was recognised as refined and cultured, and it
was possible for the people to model their speech after this.

Most of the materials in this book were supplied by great men
and women of Busiro county. Its history has remained intact
because [here the most of the wives and servants of the deceased
kings stayed.] If a wife died the clan had to supply another woman
to take her place and she took the name of the deceased.

The people were rich. They had plenty of goats, barkcloth, and
cattle. All the districts were well populated. There was not much
raising of plantains and bananas, but there was much cultivation of
sweet potatoes, yams, sugar cane, and fruits. Famine was never felt
here as severely as in other parts of the country. The Bulam
district was particularly noted for cattle raising.

[Mugema was chief of the country since time immemorial,] and
only twice was he deposed, each time to be reinstated. [He belonged to the Ŋkima clan.] (253)

Mawokota county.

This was a favorite county with the Baganda because each clan
had property here. In the old days several kings established their
capitals here.

The people developed a nice manner of speaking because they
were accustomed to speak with their gods, on whom they depended in
all their undertakings.

Bananas, plantains, potatoes, and so forth were plentiful. They
made a beer from bananas which was noted for its strength. They
were also rich in barkcloth, cattle and goats. Kakinda of the Kobe
clan, Sebwato of the Mamba clan, Semandwa and Kabogoza of
the Ŋonge clan, were the barkcloth producers. (These, with others,
Roscoe lists as district sub-chiefs.) (254)

Some of the best pastures were Kikera near the Katoŋga river,
which is like a small island, because the river curves along one side,
and Lwera Plain, in which there are many rivers, on the other. Here
the fishing trade was highly developed too. The large rivers,
Nakyetema, Kaluŋgi, Nawandege, and Kibukuta, took several
hours to cross.

Busudju County.

Busudju was the county in which Kintu first made his official
residence. Here he founded Nono city at Magoŋga, where he died.

At the ascension to the throne of Kimera the Saza chief Kadjubi was assigned to the leadership of this county. Mutebi removed him and made it an office of the Lugave clan. This clan was honored because of its position as [guardian to the children of the king. Kasudju was accordingly honored before all the Saza chiefs.] (256) There is a proverb expressive of this, "Busudju is better than Butambala." This originated in connection with the court held by Kasudju to settle the problems of the princes and princesses......

There were several good pasture lands in this county; Budjubi, Ŋkazebuka, Galwe, and Manyi. There were also places which yielded a rich harvest. There were no cow diseases, but a great many terrifying wild animals.

Kyawaŋgabo was another good place. The pasturing was very agreeable due to the warmth of the climate. It was sub-divided into a great many small holdings. But the place was somehow not very popular and was accordingly not very populous.

There are two large rivers, Kiteŋga and Kasa. At the time of completing this volume there had been a reorganization and this part of the land had been divided and transferred to two other counties.

Budu County.

[This county, which was founded by Djundju, was separate from the others.] (255) The inhabitants were known as Banabudu. These people were particularly adept at serving in chief's courts. In the old days the people of Budu used to give large presents to their chiefs so that they would be liked. The county was very rich and the people very vain of their wealth. They did not like a poor person to use the same beer-jug which they used. This county is very near Aŋkole and had therefore several kinds of cattle, goats and sheep. They also produced the fine red barkcloth.

The county was divided into several parts, each having a particular specialty. Mawogola, Bwera, and Kadjumba were for pasturing. The barkcloths were made at Saŋgo, and known as Saŋgo barkcloths. Some were also made at Budjadju. Fishing was done particularly at Buyaga. The members of the Tailless Cow clan were blacksmiths and made all sorts of things, from knives to spears. They became the best blacksmiths because they knew how to extract the iron from the ores. Lubyai, a Ŋgabi clan chief, was noted for his artistic dyeing. He produced barkcloths resembling cotton in patterning.

There was a beer known as Kibombo made in Budu. This name is that of an undrinkable bitter grass. There were many plantain and coffee plantations. The largest rivers in Budu are Nabadjuzi, Naludugavu, Kyogya, and Tero, which is partly surrounded by a wood. Budu is not a very healthy county. There is prevalent a children's disease which is characterised by severe abdominal pain, and there are ticks and mosquitoes.

Gomba County.

This was founded by Katenga. [It is near Singo] and the people were much like those of this county. The parts most pleasant to live in were Ekitabuza and Kakubansiri, which have the [healthiest and most fattening pastures.] (255) Empendja was a wild place and Matonga a hill noted chiefly for the death there by plague of Suna returning from war. Kyawangabo was a part containing Kasozi hill where Mugalula, the father of the Nsenene clan, ruled absolutely in the old days. Here there are good pastures and two rivers, Kabasuma and Kibimba, which originate in Wamala Lake. The highest hill is Ngomanene.

Butambala County.

This also was founded by Katerega. It is in the center with reference to the other counties. The people resembled those of Mawokota. The Ndiga clan headed this county until the reign of Mwanga, when it was turned over to Taibu Magato of the Musu clan. The people were active and intelligent as those of Busudju and Mawokota. There are no large rivers or hills. One part, Kiwala, near Katonga river, is good pasturage. There the king's shepherds Magango and Lukenku used to be. The land was mostly owned by clan landlords except for Kirema, Kitimba, and Kitaulira, where the ordinary man could own land.....

Buwekula County.

This was originally part of Bunyoro. During the reign of Kamanya, Kiwalabye of the Kobe clan fought and conquered the Banyoro, obtaining this land for Buganda. He then became chief of it and founded his court at Kabyuma hill. Later he was appointed Sabawali of Singo county, and was known as Luwekula. This name was given him by the natives of the place. At first they used to run away from him and always carried their children with them on their backs. At a certain hour they would say "Bring down the children to suck. It is very bad, this Muganda is after us." This went on until they gave him the nickname. Before that Mubende hill had been known as Mubende of Bugaŋgazi. Kawaŋga side was known as Mweŋge. In 1892 Sepiriya Mutagwanya was appointed to this post. In 1893 the county was unified.

Koki County.

[Kamuswaga, even though he was under the jurisdiction of the Buganda kingdom, was nevertheless a petty king in his territory.] (234)

Kabaka Sansa Gabigogo of Banyoro was the father of three children — Luhaga I, Sansa II, and Bwawe. Later on the elderly king died and his eldest child, Luhaga I, succeeded him. Luhaga I became very bitter and hated all his brothers. Bwawe took the initiative; he left the country and made his way to the Aŋkole tribe. Later on Bwawe led a siege against Koki county and when he reached there he found that the natives were a peace loving people. He therefore sent word to his brother Luhaga I to allow him to make his home in that country. "Sir, why don't you allow me to remain in this country? I shall bring you riches from here." Luhaga I granted his brother's request. Then Bwawe had his mother Ndagano remain in Koki, while he himself accompanied his brother Luhaga I back to Banyoro, and then returned to the Koki country. When Bwawe came back to Koki he became a law unto himself. His children were Kiteimbwa, Mudjwiga, Mugeni, and Ndaula. Formerly Koki belonged to Kaziransomo, king of Kiziba, whom Bwawe ousted. When Bwawe died his oldest son Kiteimbwa succeeded him. Kiteimbwa fought with the Baganda people. He defeated them and took as loot most of their spears. He took the booty to his grandfather Luhaga to show him how he had fought bravely and defeated the Baganda tribe. When Luhaga's men saw this they were very much concerned and advised him that unless he checked his grandson's popularity he himself was doomed to death or dethronement. "It is better," they told him "to arrest this grandson of yours and kill him. Because of the strength and popularity he gained by his victory over the Baganda, he will eventually turn against you and you will suffer." Luhaga listened to the advice of his people and killed his grandson. While Kiteimbwa was being led to his death, he said, "Never let my brothers who succeed me come over to Bunyoro, but let them annex their kingdom to that of the Baganda."

When Mudjwiga succeeded his father, he sent word to Djundju that he had annulled his connection with the Bunyoro kingdom. "I am no longer under the government of Bunyoro kingdom", Kabaka Kiteimbwa told Djundju, "I want to be under your protection. It will also be fitting if you could send men so that we can fight against the Banyoro people who have found a foothold in Budu country." Djundju designated Luzige of the Ndiga clan to go and make war against the Banyoro people in Budu. He went, fought, and conquered over them. Luzige was appointed [Pokino, under whom the Kabaka was ruled and protected.] (234) When Mudjwiga died, he was succeeded by his brother Ndaula I. Ndaula was succeeded by his son Kiteimbwa II, who was succeeded by his son Sansa II, who was in turn succeeded by his son Lubambula. Lubambula was succeeded by his brother Kamuswaga Ndaula II. This last king was a very nice man. During the Christian-Mohammedan warfare in 1888 he protected the Christians.

In 1894 he consented to be the first county chief according to the laws of Buganda. He filled all the important positions in the county with men who had fought side by side with him in his campaigns. He died after he had been baptized with the name Kozhia. He was succeeded by his son Sifasi Djodje Sansa Kabumbuli.

Kabula County.

Kabula was formerly Aŋkole territory. In 1888 there broke out a war between the Christians and the Mohammedans. The Christians fled to Aŋkole. Kabaka Ntale asked the fleeing band where they wanted to make their homes. "We like Kabula, that hilly place," they replied. They chose this place because they were sure of cultivating plantain there. Ntale then consented to their request. On October 5th, 1889, the Christians defeated the Mohammedan forces and returned to Buganda.

When the Christians left the county, Ntale gave it to other Baganda people who were opium users. These people became very disturbing. They refused to heed either Ntale or the King of Buganda. Then the Baganda kingdom demanded an assurance from Ntale that he was not planning to war against them. "Are you going to war against us," the Baganda people inquired, "since your subjects are insulting us so badly ?" But he denied any knowledge of existing hostility against the Baganda, and asked the King of Buganda to war against the rebels. Finally the Baganda fought and won: with the consent of the British government it was annexed to the Buganda kingdom in October, 1899, as the province of Lumanma. Saulo Mayandja of the Lugave clan was made chief; he was succeeded by Amoni Bazira, who was later transferred to Bunyoro, and then by Musa Sebalu of the Mamba clan.

Buyaga County.

Buyaga was formerly Banyoro territory. In 1896 when the British government battled against Kaberega, King of Bunyoro, the Baganda people helped in the war. In return for their service, the government offered them that territory. Then it was known as Kyambalaŋgo County. Firidina Mabaŋga of the Mamba clan was appointed. He continued in this office until Kabaka Daudi Tcwa assumed the throne. Noli Ndadji, and later Nyasi Lule succeeded him.

Bululi County.

Bululi was formerly a territory of the king of Bunyoro. It was then occupied by the following chiefs — Banda, Kabagambe, Kadoma, Kadyebo, Muteŋgesa and princess Naŋgoma. In 1896 the British government, during the reign of Mwaŋga II, annexed it to Buganda kingdom. Then it was divided among the following honorable chiefs. — Apolo Kagwa, Matayo Mudjasi, Zakaliya Kizito, Paulo Nsubuga, Djoswa Kate, and Yona Waswa. They erected fortresses to protect it from enemies. On May 9, 1898, the territory was made a county. Andereya Luwandaga of the Mamba clan was appointed as Kimbugwe.

Bugerere County.

This was also Bunyoro territory, occupied by Namuyondjo. It was added to Buganda by the British government on October 25, 1895. When Semei Kakuŋgulu of the Mamba clan resigned as Kimbugwe when Mwaŋga II was king, he went and made his home in Bugerere until 1899 when he left for the Bakedi county. In 1900 Daudi Tcwa made it a county. Matayo Nsubuga was then appointed chief; Temuseo Kivebulaya Mulondo of the Mpindi clan, formerly Sabawali of Sekibobo, became assistant Mugerere. Serwano Mazinga of the Kasimba clan succeeded him in 1905.

Bugaŋgazi County.

Bugaŋgazi was formerly a part of Bugaya. In 1900, the king made it a separate county. Anserimi Kiwanuka of the Nsenene clan was appointed Kiimba. Aleni Kinanina followed him. He had been a soldier and was later killed during the Great War.

Mawagola County.

Mawagola was formerly owned by a man named Mpandju of Bwera origin. At one time he was at the head of two governments, that of Buganda and that of Aŋkole. His people were engaged in the salt industry. In 1900 it was made a separate county. Andereya Kiwanuka of the Mbogo clan was appointed Mutesa, and minor chiefs were appointed. His successors were Nyasi Lule, Semeo Nsubuga, Mamba clan; Aleni Kinanina; Yozefu Sebowa, Kasimbi clan.

Sese County.

Sese county is composed of several islands in Lake Victoria. In 1900 Yosiya Kasozi was appointed chief. All minor chieftainships were filled with inhabitants of the islands.

Sese has always belonged to Buganda. It supplied boats for the navy, and houses all the great oracles. The chief value of the land was in its fishing. It was owned by the queen mother, prime minister, treasurer, Nanzigu, Lubaga and Mukwenda.

Buvuma County.

Buvuma was also composed of several islands. The inhabitants remained independent for several years. They were known as Bagwe and Baziŋga, but had no king. Djuko's brother conquered and ruled them, but was later removed. The Sekibobo subdued them. Then they were enraged and said, "This lifeless slender fellow with sharpened teeth has conquered us." Thus they got their name, which means "Abusers". They were conquered in 1893. In 1900 Nova Naluswa, Ŋkima clan, was appointed chief. He was followed by Yozefu Kiwanuka Nsiŋgisira, Butiko clan.

CHAPTER XXXVI

THE POMP OF THE KING OF BUGANDA.

The following account gives an idea of the pomp of the King of Buganda and of his power in governing. When the king was about to appear, that is, to open the parliament, there was an overwhelming display. All people who were in their houses remained indoors; those in the street kneeled down; and all the drums, trumpets, and every sounding instrument was used to proclaim his majesty's approach. There was a band of executioners who walked near his majesty, ready to imprison and if necessary to kill any person who was found guilty of any sort of offense. When a verdict was passed in the parliament, the guilty person was quickly enveloped in a multitude of ropes; even if he tried to plead for mercy, it was impossible that his majesty should hear him because he was almost choked to death.

There were many who, in order to gain recognition, told lies about other chiefs, so that they might lose their offices. It was not until Mutesa that that kind of system was done away with. When one person accused another, the king sent for the accused person and told him that such and such a thing had been said about him. Mutesa was against people who told him untruths. He demanded the truth of the accused. If the man was guilty and told the truth, he was soon acquitted. If he lied and witnesses were produced who certified as to his guilt, he was finally killed.

When the king walked for exercise, there were many people about him. If he came to a place where there was no road, the people soon made one for him. During his journeys, all door-keepers were required to carry their doors with them. When the king rested, they enclosed him with the doors and guarded him. To understand the kingly power it should be said that he was a law unto himself, an absolute monarch. The following were the king's palace officers. (Some of these check with those mentioned by Roscoe, whose list is, however, not complete.)

Kauta	Chef
Seruti	Butler
Kaula	Drummer
Nsandja	King's priest, who guarded all his horns.
Banda	Potter
Omukweya	King's head carrier during the journeys
Omusoloza	Man in charge of fire wood.

There was also the executioner's division. All these and many other petty divisions made up the king's household and contributed to his pomp. Sabakaki was the title of a person who was the head of the king's palace, including the division of the king's pages. He was promptly obeyed in everything he said. In the division of the king's pages there were about one thousand young men appointed by various chiefs to serve his majesty in the palace. They were under a chief named Sabawali.

Next to the king came his prime minister. He too was honored. When his drums sounded, all chiefs hurried to his palace to go with him to the king's court. The prime minister walked very slowly to give the people a chance to join him. When he reached the court he sat down to render judgment. When the king appeared to open the court, the prime minister presented the cases. Those who appealed to his majesty were given a chance to present their own cases. The prime minister had two assistants to help him dispose of the cases. One assistant was in Masengere and the other in Gombolola in the outer royal court. The communication between his majesty and the prime minister was carried on by means of constant messengers, a man and a woman from the prime minister and a messenger from the king. The prime minister's messengers kept the king acquainted with what was going on in the country at large and the king's messenger kept the prime minister informed of the latest decisions or suggestions or new decrees issued by the king. Oftentimes there was concerted action, for they respected each other. If the king wished to do anything or to order something from his estates, the word went through the prime minister. The prime minister's messenger working with the king's messenger were certain to bring anything from any part of the country, but one without the other could do nothing.

All chiefs, high or low, when they visited the capital, brought news, or something to give to the king. First they reported to the prime minister and got his assent. All secrets to be told the king went through the prime minister, and vice versa. When the king decided to appoint another prime minister, he stopped the prime minister's reception of all important and secret messages. Instead he designated Kimbugwe, the king's twin guard, to receive information concerning state affairs pending the appointment of the new prime minister. When the new prime minister was to be charged with state affairs,..... the king stood outside the parliament house with his scepter; a group of chiefs selected as candidates faced him. Then the king gave his scepter to the man he designated as prime minister, saying, "Go and judge my Buganda country." The newly appointed chief repeated the oath of allegiance, saying, "I shall render justice." After which he left and entered his official residence and the king returned to his palace. The prime minister never gave thanks or knelt down as did other chiefs.

All Saza chiefs were equally powerful in their respective counties. No messenger of whatever nature could travel in a county without a Saza chief's messenger to accompany him. If the king's and the prime minister's messengers were sent to Muwemba to assist Mukwenda in buying cows for the king, they couldn't bring anything unless they had with them a Saza chief's messenger. They were regarded as thieves. This is one point to show how well Buganda was governed. The Baganda, as far back as can be remembered, have been an obedient and well-governed people, respecting their king, chiefs, and country. (Chapter 23) This may account for the respect and encouragement with which the British Government has consented to regard the native system of government.

List of Names.

The following list comprises all the native terms which were retained in the translation, in a form which attempts more accurately to represent the phonetics. Particular attention has been paid to tone, which is very important in Luganda. *1*, *2*, and *3*, written below the line and following vowels or consonants represent respectively their pitch, low, middle, and high; a notation such as *21* means a glide from middle towards low. Length, of vowel or consonant, has been indicated by a point above the line, and accents indicate such stressed syllables as are very marked. '*b* indicates a more plosive sound than *b*, which is really a bilabial continuant. There is considerable inaccuracy in the recording of the labials, as greater attention was paid at first to the question of tone. It was impossible to revise these later because of the departure of Mr. Kalibala.

My informant was occasionally uncertain as to pronunciation of a name. Alternative versions have been written in brackets.

Most of the words in this list are proper names. (*w*) after one means that it is exclusively female. An attempt has been made to indicate those which are not personal names. *Off*, indicates the name of an office or functioning group; *Tr*, the name — appearing in either the singular or plural — of a local group or distinct tribe; *Ph*, merely a word difficult to translate, or a colloquial phrase, such as a nickname; and *Cl*, a clan. Christian and Mohammedan names are italicized. Prefixes have been retained throughout.

A

$A_2ba_2djo_2na_2$ Off potters 94

$A_1ba_1ka'_2ndja_2$ Off beermakers 156

$A_1ba_1ke'_2be_2zi_2$ Off 73

$A_1ba_1ku_2nta_{21}$ Off militia 39

$A_1ba_1nywa'_2$ Off beermakers 73

$A_1ba_2pe'_2re_2$ Off wrestlers 147

$A_1'ba_1sam_2'ba_2z·i_1$ Off 150

$A_1ba_1te·_2te_1$ Off musicians 95

$A_1'ba'_2vu_2ma_2$ Tr 29, 158, 163

$A_1'ba_2yu_2ndju_3$ Tr 38

$A_2bi_2sa_2dji_1$ 52 (w)

$A_2d·o_2lo_2ni·_2ka_2$ ($A_2d·o'_2 lo_2ni·_2ka_1$) 59, 60, 61

$A_1ga'_2ti_1$ 60

$A_2gi_1ri'_2$ (w) 53

$A_1ka_2ba'_2na·_2ku_2lya'_1$ Ph a nickname 143

$A_1la_1ma_1za'_2ne_1$ 61

$A'_2le_1ni_1$ 170

$A_1li_2ba_2ta_2kya_2ye_{21}$ (w) 44

$A_1li_2bu_1li_2ra_2$ (w) 44

$A_1li_2ki'_2si_1$ 59, 60, 66

$A_1li_2ndji_2dju'_2ki_1ra_1$ (w) 54

$A_1li'_2rwa$ (w) 60

M

M_1'pe$_2$t·a$_2$ Pl 75
M_1pe'$_2$wo$_2$ Cl (oribi) 10.., 44.., 84
M_1pi'$_2$ma$_1$ Ph dagger 28
M_1pi'$_3$me$_1$re$_2$be$_2$ra$_2$ 82
M_1pi'$_2$n$_1$di$_2$ Cl (seed) 26, 38, 42..., 54, 104
M_1pi'$_2$ŋga$_2$ 13, 26, 34, 64, 85, 162
M_1pi$_2$si$_1$ '
M_1po'$_2$lo$_2$go'$_2$ma$_2$ Cl (lion) 26, 45 54
M_1po$_1$ma'$_2$ Pl 163
M_1po'$_2$za$_2$ki$_2$ 41
M_1pu$_2$mu$_1$de$_2$ Pl 21, 117
M_1pu$_2$mu$_1$la$_1$ 122
M_1pu·$_2$ŋ$_1$gu$_{21}$ 27
Mu$_1$'ba'$_2$ŋgo$_2$ Pl 10
Mu$_1$ba$_1$ta'$_2$ŋge$_1$ 'Bu$_1$ka'$_2$zi$_1$ Ph 104
Mu$_1$be'$_2$nde$_2$ Pl 122, 166
Mu$_1$bi$_2$ŋge$_1$ Pl 69
Mu$_1$bi$_1$ru'$_2$ 10, 56, 123
Mu$_1$bi'$_2$si$_1$ (w) 46, 71, 153
Mu$_1$byo$_2$wu$_2$wo'$_{21}$ 41
Mu$_1$d·ja'$_3$gu$_2$zo$_2$ Ph drum 28, 57, 65, 75, 85, 117.., 145
Mu$_1$dja'$_2$m$_2$bu$_2$la$_2$ 85
Mu$_1$dja'$_2$si$_2$ 169
Mu$_1$djo'$_2$be$_1$ 122
Mu$_1$dju'$_2$m'bu$_2$la$_2$ 86, 113
Mu$_1$djwi'$_2$ga$_1$ 168
Mu$_1$do$_2$ndo$_2$li$_1$ 49
Mu'$_2$fu$_1$mu'$_2$la$_2$ 154
Mu$_1$g·a'$_2$be$_2$ 19
Mu$_1$sa$_2$dja$_1$ga$_1$lu$_1$nya'$_2$go$_2$ Ph 57
Mu$_1$ga$_1$le'$_2$ 49, 53
Mu$_1$ga'$_2$lu$_2$ 86
Mu$_1$ga'$_2$lu$_3$la$_3$ (Mu$_1$ga'$_2$lu$_2$la$_2$) 19, 86, 166
Mu$_1$ga'$_2$m'be$_1$ 153
Mu$_1$ga'$_2$n$_2$da$_1$ Tr 9, 16, 19, 146
Mu$_1$ga'$_2$ŋga$_2$ 153
Mu$_1$ga$_2$nza$_2$bu$_2$li$_1$rwa$_1$ (w) 46
Mu$_1$ga$_2$n·za$_2$ma$_2$la$_2$ku$_2$wo$_2$na$_1$ (w) 46
Mu$_1$ga$_2$n·zi'r$_2$wa$_2$za$_1$ (w) 46, 50
Mu$_1$ge'$_2$ma$_2$ Off 12..., 27, 31, 41...., 53..., 63.., 75, 83, 90, 108
Mu$_1$ge'$_2$ni$_2$ 167
Mu$_1$ge'$_2$ra$_2$ Pl 155
Mu$_1$ge$_2$re'$_2$ŋge$_2$djo'$_2$ 105
Mugerere 169
Mu$_1$gi'$_2$ŋga$_2$ 157
Mu$_1$go'$_3$'ba$_3$ 86
Mu$_1$go$_2$go$_2$

Mu$_1$go$_2$lo'$_{21}$ba$_1$ (w) 53, 68
Mu$_1$go$_2$m'ba$_2$ 46
Mu$_1$go'$_2$ŋga$_2$ 38
Mu$_1$g·u'$_2$la$_2$ 48, 61, 153
Mu$_1$g·u'$_2$lu$_2$ka$_2$ 28
Mu$_1$gu'$_2$lu$_2$ma$_2$ 43, 59, 61
Mu$_1$gwa'$_2$nya$_2$ 34, 35, 60
Mu$_1$i'$_2$ma$_2$ (Mu$_1$hi'$_2$ma$_1$) Tr 16, 46, 97, 104
Mu$_1$i'$_2$nda$_2$ 46, 61
Mu$_1$i'$_2$ra$_1$ 155
Mu·$_2$ka$_1$ 58
Mu$_1$k·a'$_2$'bya$_2$ 14..., 19, 45, 50..., 68, 78..., 84.., 97, 116, 145...
Mu$_1$ka$_2$ka'$_2$ Pl 153, 155
Mu$_1$ka'$_2$la$_1$zi$_2$ 153
Mu$_1$ka$_2$lo$_2$ Ph 30
Mu$_1$ka'$_2$m'ba$_2$ta$_2$ 69
Mu$_1$ka'$_2$sa$_2$ 9, 30, 57..., 66, 81.., 114..., 120, 125
Mu$_1$ka'$_2$ya$_2$ 120
Mu$_1$ke'$_2$ba$_1$ 45
Mu$_1$ke'$_2$be$_2$zi$_1$ 69
Mu$_1$ke'$_2$ŋgo$_1$ (w) 54
Mu$_1$ke'$_2$ra$_1$ 69
Mu$_1$ki'$_3$bi$_1$
Mu$_1$ki'$_2$ndi$_1$ki$_1$ra$_1$ 54
Mu$_1$ki$_1$ta'$_2$go$_2$bwa$_1$ Pl 119
Mu$_2$ko$_2$ke$_2$ra'$_{21}$ 41
Mu$_1$ko$_3$ki$_3$ 41
Mu$_1$ko'$_2$mul$_2$wa$_2$nyi$_2$ (w) 54
Mu$_1$ko'$_2$mu$_1$ta$_2$nda$_1$ (w) 53
Mu$_1$ko'$_2$mwe·$_2$i$_2$dzi$_1$ (w) 74
Mu$_1$ko'$_2$ta$_1$nyi$_1$ 154
Mu$_1$ku'$_2$de$_2$ Ph 54
Mu$_1$ku'$_2$lu$_1$ a$_1$ta$_1$ma$_1$ka'$_2$ge$_1$ Ph 58
Mu$_1$ku$_2$lu$_2$kya$_2$yo$_2$ge$_2$ra$_1$ (w) 46
Mu$_1$ku$_1$lwa$_2$li$_1$ma$_1$nyi$_1$ka$_1$ (also canoe) 155
Mu$_1$k·u'$_2$ma$_1$ 28, 38, 45, 54, 48
Mu$_1$ku$_2$ndja$_2$ 45
Mu$_1$ku$_1$sa'$_2$ 39
Mu$_1$ku$_1$su'$_2$ 26, 48, 68, 157
Mu$_1$kwa'$_2$ku$_2$la$_2$ 69
Mu$_1$kwa'$_2$no$_1$ Ph friendship 41
Mu$_1$kwa$_2$no$_2$gwe$_2$nya'$_2$ndja$_1$ (also canoe) 154
Mu$_1$kwa'$_2$nya$_2$ 69
Mu$_1$kwe'$_2$nda$_2$ Off 20, 24, 28, 44, 59, 64, 68, 75, 143, 158, 170.
Mu$_2$kwe'$_2$ya$_1$ 69

COLUMBIA UNIVERSITY
CONTRIBUTIONS TO ANTHROPOLOGY ·

Edited by
FRANZ BOAS
Professor of Anthropology
Columbia University

COLUMBIA UNIVERSITY PRESS
Columbia University
New York

Foreign Agent
OXFORD UNIVERSITY PRESS
Humphrey Milford
Amen House, London, E. C.

Date Due

9 781014 703071